MICROSOFT SHAREPOINT USER GUIDE 2026 EDITION

BUILD, SHARE, AND MANAGE TEAM PROJECTS SEAMLESSLY ACROSS YOUR ORGANIZATION

ETHAN J. COLLINS

DISCLAIMER

The information provided in this guide is intended for educational and informational purposes only. While every effort has been made to ensure the accuracy and completeness of the content, **Microsoft SharePoint**, **Microsoft 365**, and related tools are continually updated, and features may change over time.

This guide does **not constitute professional, legal, or financial advice**, and the author or publisher cannot be held responsible for any errors, omissions, or outcomes resulting from the use of this guide. Users are encouraged to consult official Microsoft documentation, support channels, or certified professionals for specific guidance tailored to their organization's needs.

Quick Tip: Always test new settings, workflows, or integrations in a safe environment before deploying them in a live production setting. This ensures your data remains secure and your operations uninterrupted.

By using this guide, you acknowledge and accept that the author and publisher are not liable for any direct or indirect consequences arising from the application of the information provided.

TABLE OF CONTENT

Chapter 1: Introduction to SharePoint

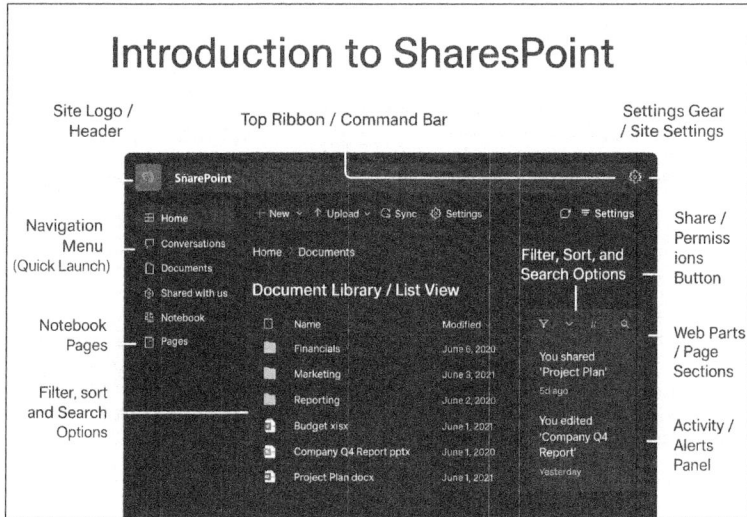

Introduction to SharesPoint

Site Logo / Header	Top Ribbon / Command Bar	Settings Gear / Site Settings

SharePoint

- Home
- Conversations
- Documents
- Shared with us
- Notebook
- Pages

+ New · ↑ Upload · ⟳ Sync · ⚙ Settings

Home > Documents

Document Library / List View

☐ Name	Modified
■ Financials	June 6, 2020
■ Marketing	June 3, 2021
■ Reporting	June 2, 2020
▣ Budget xlsx	June 1, 2021
▣ Company Q4 Report.pptx	June 1, 2020
▣ Project Plan.docx	June 1, 2021

⟲ ≡ Settings

Filter, Sort, and Search Options

▽ · ⫶ 🔍

You shared 'Project Plan' 5d ago

You edited 'Company Q4 Report' Yesterday

- Navigation Menu (Quick Launch)
- Notebook Pages
- Filter, sort and Search Options

- Share / Permissions Button
- Web Parts / Page Sections
- Activity / Alerts Panel

1.1 What SharePoint Is and Why It Matters

A simple way to think about SharePoint

SharePoint is a platform Microsoft built to help organizations store documents, share information, and run lightweight applications that support day-to-day teamwork. At its core, SharePoint starts with sites and libraries where files live, but it grows into something much bigger: a company-wide hub for collaboration, knowledge, and business processes. For many teams, SharePoint replaces messy shared drives, scattered email attachments, and lost versions of documents with a single, searchable place that keeps work connected and traceable. If you have ever struggled to find the latest version of a file, wished your team could collaborate in real time, or wanted a secure place to publish policies and procedures, SharePoint is designed to solve those problems.

Why SharePoint matters for modern work

SharePoint matters because it turns files and information into living assets rather than static clutter. When documents are stored in SharePoint, they become easy to find through search and metadata, you can see who changed what and when through version history, and teams can co-author documents simultaneously without crossing wires. SharePoint also integrates with Microsoft 365 services like Teams, Outlook, OneDrive, and Power Platform, which means your content can move naturally between chat, email, tasks, and automation. For managers and leaders, SharePoint provides oversight and governance: permissions, auditing, and retention policies help the organisation meet security and compliance needs while empowering staff with the right access.

How SharePoint fits into everyday workflows

Imagine a typical project: kickoff emails, planning documents, spreadsheets for budgets, and status updates sent by different people. Without a central place, those items scatter across inboxes and local folders. With SharePoint, the project has a dedicated site where meeting notes, timelines, task lists, and documents are collected and organized. Team members access the site from their browser or via Microsoft Teams, edit Word and Excel files directly in the browser or in the desktop apps, and use SharePoint pages to publish project status summaries. Work that used to be fragmented becomes an organized stream, and newcomers can catch up quickly by reading the site's pages and viewing the document library rather than sifting through old emails.

Who benefits from SharePoint and how

SharePoint is useful to a wide range of users across an organization. Individual contributors benefit from reliable storage, version control, and easy sharing. Team leads appreciate the ability to centralize documentation and coordinate tasks. IT and compliance teams gain tools to enforce policies, manage site lifecycle, and audit activity. Executives benefit from company intranets built on SharePoint that provide centralized communications, announcements, and dashboards. Even non-technical staff find it accessible because most common tasks—uploading files, creating a page, or sharing a link—are straightforward and supported by helpful templates and integrated apps.

What makes SharePoint different from a shared drive

A shared drive is essentially a digital filing cabinet: folders and files with limited metadata, few safeguards, and little in the way of search intelligence. SharePoint, by contrast, adds structure and context. Files in SharePoint can include metadata—descriptive tags that make it much easier to filter and find content. SharePoint supports version history, so you can roll back to an earlier draft if needed. Permissions in SharePoint are granular and auditable, so you can control who sees or edits sensitive content. Search in SharePoint indexes not only filenames but also the content within documents, pages, and lists, which drastically reduces the time spent hunting for information. In short, SharePoint is a searchable, governed, and integrated replacement for the limitations of a plain shared drive.

How SharePoint supports knowledge management

Knowledge management is about capturing institutional memory so future teams don't repeat the same mistakes. SharePoint shines here because it lets organizations publish structured content such as policies, procedures, FAQs, and how-to guides on SharePoint pages. These pages can be organized into hubs and sites, linked to each other, and surfaced through search. Because content can be assigned owners and review dates, knowledge stays current. SharePoint also supports content types—standardized templates for things like contracts, project plans, or meeting notes—ensuring consistency across the organization. Teams can add rich media like images and videos, embed forms for feedback, and build simple workflows that move knowledge through review and approval stages.

Security, governance, and compliance: why they matter in SharePoint

One reason many organizations choose SharePoint is the security model and governance capabilities. SharePoint integrates with Microsoft's security stack for authentication, conditional access, and identity management. Permissions can be set at multiple levels—site, library, folder, or item—so you can limit access where needed. For compliance, SharePoint supports retention policies, eDiscovery, and audit logs that help meet legal and regulatory obligations. Administrators can apply governance policies to control site provisioning, lifecycle, and external sharing. For organizations handling sensitive data, these controls are essential because they balance the need for collaboration with the need to protect confidential information.

How SharePoint enables process automation and low-code solutions

SharePoint is not just a place for documents; it's a platform where simple business processes can be automated. Using Power Automate, teams can create workflows that move documents through approval stages, send reminders, or automatically update fields when conditions change. SharePoint lists act as lightweight databases where records are stored and tracked, and Power Apps can surface custom forms and mobile-friendly interfaces for data entry. This low-code ecosystem means that teams without advanced developer skills can automate recurring tasks and create tailored solutions, dramatically reducing manual work and improving consistency.

Real-world examples to make it concrete

Consider a human resources team onboarding new employees. SharePoint can host an onboarding site with forms to collect employee details, checklists for IT setup, links to training resources, and a calendar for orientation sessions. Automations can trigger welcome emails, create IT tickets, and assign training tasks. Another example is a facilities team that uses a SharePoint list to log maintenance requests; technicians update the list as they work, and SharePoint pages display real-time dashboards of open issues. A marketing team might use SharePoint to manage campaign assets, store brand guidelines, and publish content calendars accessible to agency partners. In each case, SharePoint reduces friction and centralizes work.

Common misconceptions and practical realities

Some people think SharePoint is only for intranets or that it is overly complex. In reality, SharePoint scales from small team sites to enterprise intranets. It includes templates and starter sites for common scenarios so teams don't have to start from scratch. Another misconception is that SharePoint replaces other tools; instead, it integrates with the tools people already use—Teams for chat and meetings, Outlook for email, and OneDrive for personal files—so users experience a cohesive environment rather than a collection of disconnected apps. Teams that plan content structure and governance up front typically find SharePoint straightforward and highly productive.

Getting started: practical first steps for teams

A practical approach to adopting SharePoint begins with identifying a single, high-impact use case such as a project site or team knowledge base. Start by creating a site with a clear purpose, add a document library, and migrate a small set of files. Set simple permissions and invite a few collaborators to test co-authoring. Experiment with a SharePoint page to publish an overview and embed a list for tracking tasks. Once the team is comfortable, iterate: add metadata, enable versioning, and set up a basic Power Automate flow for approvals. Small, visible wins build confidence and momentum across the organization.

Measuring success and continuous improvement

Measure success by tracking adoption metrics such as site visits, document activity, search queries, and task completion rates. Solicit user feedback to identify usability gaps and adjust navigation or content organization. Over time, establish a content owner model so every site and library has a responsible person who maintains relevance and accuracy. Keep governance light but clear: define who can create sites, how long sites remain active, and rules for external sharing. Continuous improvement and periodic audits keep the SharePoint environment healthy and aligned with business needs.

Pro tip: Start with a single, clearly defined pilot site and use it as a learning environment. Don't try to migrate everything at once; incremental changes reduce risk and create opportunities to refine your structure and governance.

Good to Know: SharePoint is most effective when paired with simple governance and training. A brief onboarding session for new users showing how to store files, share links, and search content often prevents common issues and accelerates adoption.

Final thought: how SharePoint creates lasting value

SharePoint's true value lies in turning scattered information into an organized, secure, and discoverable resource that supports ongoing work. When teams use SharePoint to centralize documents, automate routine processes, and share knowledge, the organization gains speed, accountability, and resilience. Over time, a well-managed

SharePoint environment becomes the connective tissue that holds distributed work together, reduces rework, and helps people spend less time hunting for files and more time doing meaningful work.

1.2 SharePoint Online vs. On-Premises

Understanding the two deployment models

SharePoint can be deployed in two main ways: **SharePoint Online** and **SharePoint On-Premises**. Both provide the core capabilities of SharePoint—sites, libraries, lists, document management, and collaboration—but they differ significantly in terms of setup, management, flexibility, cost, and integration. Choosing the right model depends on your organization's technical capabilities, security requirements, budget, and long-term goals.

SharePoint Online: Cloud-Based Convenience

What it is:

SharePoint Online is part of Microsoft 365, meaning your SharePoint environment is hosted on Microsoft's cloud servers. You don't have to maintain your own infrastructure, and updates are automatic. You access it through a web browser, desktop apps, or mobile apps from virtually anywhere.

Why organizations love it:

- **Low maintenance:** Microsoft handles all server maintenance, updates, and security patches. Your IT team can focus on governance, user support, and business processes rather than servers.
- **Always up-to-date:** Features and improvements are rolled out continuously without manual upgrades. This means you get the latest capabilities like improved search, AI-powered content suggestions, and integration with Teams, Power Automate, and Power Apps.
- **Accessibility:** Employees can access SharePoint Online from any device with an internet connection. Remote work and hybrid work models are naturally supported.
- **Integrated ecosystem:** SharePoint Online is tightly connected with other Microsoft 365 apps, such as Teams, Outlook, OneDrive, Power Platform, and Office apps. This creates seamless workflows between collaboration, communication, and automation.

Examples of usage:

- A marketing team shares campaign files and collaborates on proposals from different locations.
- HR hosts an onboarding portal accessible to new hires worldwide.
- Project teams track tasks in SharePoint lists integrated with Teams channels.

Quick Tip: Don't worry if your team isn't highly technical—SharePoint Online is designed to be user-friendly, and templates for team sites and communication sites make setup quick and intuitive.

SharePoint On-Premises: Local Control

What it is:

SharePoint On-Premises is installed and maintained on your organization's own servers. Your IT team manages everything: server setup, updates, backups, security, and disaster recovery.

Why some organizations choose it:

- **Full control:** You determine when updates happen, how servers are configured, and what security policies are in place. This can be critical for organizations with strict data sovereignty or regulatory requirements.
- **Customization flexibility:** On-premises installations allow deep customization and the ability to run legacy applications or highly specific workflows that may not be possible in the cloud.
- **Offline accessibility:** Data resides in your local environment, which can be advantageous if internet connectivity is limited or unreliable.

Examples of usage:

- A government agency with strict compliance rules keeps sensitive data on local servers.
- A financial institution requires full control over user access and audit logs.
- A company needs complex integrations with legacy systems that are difficult to replicate in the cloud.

Watch Out For: On-premises environments require more technical expertise and ongoing maintenance. Server downtime, patch management, and storage scaling are all the responsibility of your IT team.

Key Differences Between Online and On-Premises

Feature	SharePoint Online	SharePoint On-Premises
Hosting	Microsoft Cloud	Local servers
Updates	Automatic, continuous	Manual, controlled by IT
Maintenance	Minimal, handled by Microsoft	Full responsibility of IT
Accessibility	Anywhere with internet	Primarily internal network; remote access requires setup
Cost Model	Subscription-based (Microsoft 365)	Capital expenditure for servers + ongoing maintenance
Customization	Limited to approved apps, add-ins, and Power Platform	Deep customization with code, legacy integrations
Security & Compliance	Microsoft-managed; complies with many standards	Full control; can implement custom policies
Scaling	Easy and elastic	Must purchase and maintain additional hardware for growth

Good to Know: Many organizations adopt a **hybrid approach**, using SharePoint Online for general collaboration and On-Premises for highly sensitive data or specialized legacy apps. This lets you enjoy the convenience of the cloud while maintaining local control where needed.

Which Should You Choose?

1. **If your organization values minimal IT maintenance and fast access to the latest features:**
   SharePoint Online is the preferred choice. It's ideal for teams that are geographically distributed or require cloud-first collaboration.

2. **If your organization needs total control over data, security, and custom workflows:**

SharePoint On-Premises may be necessary. This is common in highly regulated industries like government, finance, and healthcare.

3. **If you need a mix:**
   A hybrid approach provides flexibility. Sensitive data stays on-premises, while general collaboration and document sharing occur in the cloud. Microsoft supports hybrid configurations that allow seamless integration between On-Premises and Online environments.

Practical Example for Context:

Imagine a multinational company with employees in multiple countries:

- **Marketing team** uses SharePoint Online to co-author campaign documents, manage shared assets, and track social media calendars in real-time.
- **Legal and compliance teams** keep sensitive contracts and client records on SharePoint On-Premises servers, ensuring they meet data residency requirements.
- Both environments can be linked for cross-team collaboration, so necessary documents can be referenced or moved securely when appropriate.

Pro Shortcut: When starting with SharePoint, you don't need to immediately decide between Online and On-Premises. Start with a pilot Online site to familiarize your team with core features. Later, evaluate if any critical workloads need On-Premises deployment.

Conclusion:
SharePoint Online offers convenience, continuous updates, and seamless integration with the Microsoft 365 ecosystem—perfect for modern, flexible work environments. SharePoint On-Premises provides control, customization, and compliance support for organizations with strict requirements. Understanding the differences helps your team make the best choice and plan your deployment strategy wisely. Remember, SharePoint is powerful in either form, and its value grows when aligned with your organization's collaboration, knowledge management, and workflow goals.

1.3 Key Features and Benefits

SharePoint is more than just a place to store files—it's a complete platform designed to improve collaboration, streamline processes, and enhance knowledge management across your organization. Understanding its key features and the benefits they bring will help you see why it's such a powerful tool.

Document Management and Version Control

SharePoint provides robust **document libraries** where you can store, organize, and manage all types of files. Each file automatically tracks **version history**, so you can see previous edits and restore earlier versions if needed. This is especially useful when multiple people are collaborating on the same document. **Quick Tip:** Think of SharePoint like a digital filing cabinet with a built-in "undo" button for every file.

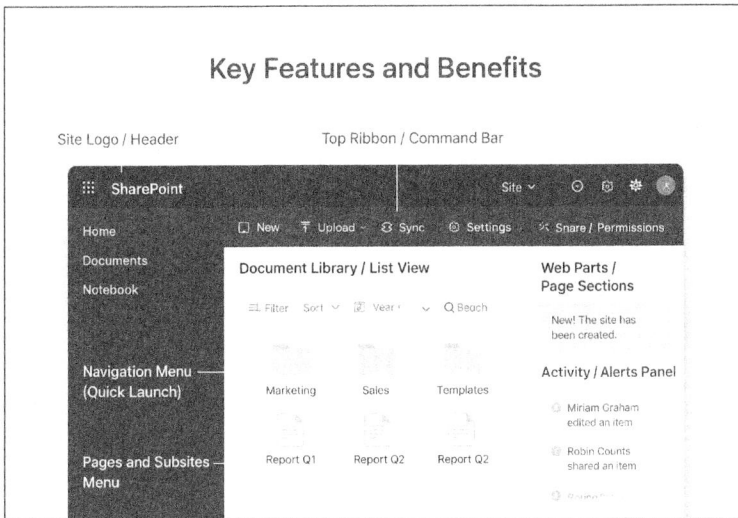

Collaboration and Co-Authoring

With SharePoint, multiple team members can **edit documents simultaneously** using Microsoft 365 apps like Word, Excel, and PowerPoint. Changes appear in real-time, reducing the need for back-and-forth emails and ensuring everyone is on the same page. You can also **leave comments** directly in documents for clearer communication. **Good to Know:** Co-authoring works seamlessly whether your colleagues are in the office, working from home, or across the globe.

Sites and Pages for Team Organization

SharePoint lets you create **team sites** and **communication sites** to organize projects, departments, or company-wide information. Team sites focus on collaboration, offering document libraries, task lists, and calendars, while communication sites are ideal for broadcasting news, updates, or resources. **Watch Out For:** Avoid cluttering your sites; plan a simple hierarchy for easy navigation.

Lists and Workflow Automation

SharePoint **lists** allow you to track tasks, contacts, issues, or inventory with customizable fields and views. You can integrate these lists with **Power Automate** to automate routine processes like approval requests, notifications, or data collection. **Pro Shortcut:** Use templates like "Issue Tracking" or "Project Tasks" to save time and maintain consistency across teams.

Search and Metadata

Finding content is easy with SharePoint's **powerful search engine**, which indexes documents, pages, and even content inside files. You can add **metadata**, such as tags or categories, to improve searchability and organize content logically. **Quick Tip:** Use descriptive titles and tags to make documents easier to find for your colleagues.

Integration with Microsoft 365 Ecosystem

SharePoint works seamlessly with **Teams, OneDrive, Outlook, Power Apps, and Power BI**. This allows you to link conversations, documents, dashboards, and apps into a unified workflow, reducing app switching and increasing efficiency. **Good to Know:** Integration enhances productivity by keeping all relevant information connected.

Security and Permissions Control

You can define **user permissions** at the site, library, folder, or file level, ensuring sensitive information is accessible only to the right people. SharePoint also supports **data loss prevention policies, encryption, and compliance features**. **Watch Out For:** Regularly review permissions to prevent outdated access or accidental data exposure.

Mobile Accessibility

SharePoint is accessible via web browsers, **desktop apps, and mobile apps**, enabling team members to work and collaborate anywhere, anytime. **Pro Shortcut:** Encourage team members to use the mobile app for quick access to documents, announcements, and tasks while on the move.

Customizable Dashboards and Web Parts

You can add **web parts** like news feeds, calendars, charts, or embedded videos to your pages, creating rich, interactive dashboards that highlight important information for your team. **Quick Tip:** Start with a few key web parts and expand gradually to avoid overwhelming users.

Benefits Summary

- **Enhanced collaboration:** Real-time co-authoring and communication reduce delays.
- **Centralized information:** One location for documents, lists, and resources.
- **Improved efficiency:** Automation reduces repetitive tasks.
- **Better knowledge management:** Search, metadata, and structured sites make content easy to find.
- **Security and compliance:** Granular permissions and Microsoft's compliance tools protect your data.
- **Flexibility:** Cloud or on-premises deployment supports diverse organizational needs.

In short, SharePoint transforms how teams **share information, collaborate, and automate processes**. It's not just a storage system; it's a central hub where your organization's knowledge, tasks, and communication come together efficiently. **Quick Tip:** Begin with a small pilot team site, explore key features like libraries, lists, and pages, and gradually expand as your team becomes comfortable with the platform.

1.4 How SharePoint Fits into Microsoft 365

SharePoint is more than just a standalone platform—it's an integral part of **Microsoft 365**, working alongside tools like Teams, OneDrive, Outlook, and Power Automate to create a seamless productivity ecosystem. Understanding how SharePoint fits within Microsoft 365 helps organizations leverage its full potential, avoid duplication, and ensure smooth collaboration across teams. Let's break it down in a friendly, practical way.

1. SharePoint as the Central Hub
Think of SharePoint as the **central nervous system** of Microsoft 365. It stores, organizes, and manages content while enabling teams to collaborate and share knowledge efficiently. While OneDrive is primarily personal storage, SharePoint acts as the **team or organizational storage space** where documents, libraries, and sites can be accessed by multiple users.

- **Example:** Imagine your marketing team is working on a campaign. OneDrive is like each team member's personal notebook, while SharePoint is the team's shared whiteboard where everyone can post updates, collaborate on content, and store reference materials.

Quick Tip: Use SharePoint for shared team documents and OneDrive for personal drafts or files not yet ready to share.

2. Integration with Microsoft Teams

Microsoft Teams is the **collaboration interface**, and SharePoint is often the engine behind it. Every Teams channel has an underlying **SharePoint document library**, meaning all files shared in Teams are actually stored in SharePoint.

- **Example:** When you upload a presentation in a Teams chat, it's stored in SharePoint. Team members can co-author the file, see version history, and access it from both Teams and SharePoint.

Good to Know: This integration means you don't have to juggle multiple platforms—Teams acts as a friendly, user-centric interface while SharePoint handles storage and document management behind the scenes.

3. Power Automate and Workflow Automation

SharePoint's integration with **Power Automate** allows you to create automated workflows that span Microsoft 365. This can save hours of repetitive tasks and ensure consistent processes.

- **Example:** Suppose HR receives a new hire request via a SharePoint form. Power Automate can automatically notify the hiring manager, create a folder in SharePoint, send an onboarding checklist via Teams, and even schedule meetings in Outlook—all automatically.

Pro Shortcut: Start with simple approvals and notifications, then gradually build more complex workflows as your comfort grows.

4. Collaboration with Office Apps

SharePoint seamlessly integrates with **Word, Excel, PowerPoint, and OneNote**. Documents stored in SharePoint can be opened, edited, and saved directly from these apps without leaving the Microsoft 365 environment. Co-authoring is smooth and real-time, reducing email attachments and version conflicts.

- **Example:** A finance team can collaborate on a quarterly budget Excel sheet, with multiple users editing simultaneously while SharePoint tracks every change.

Quick Tip: Encourage your team to use the **"Open in Desktop App"** feature for heavy-duty editing while still saving changes to SharePoint automatically.

5. Search and Knowledge Management

SharePoint's integration with **Microsoft Search** means that content stored across the Microsoft 365 ecosystem—Teams, OneDrive, Outlook, and SharePoint itself—is **easily discoverable**. This makes it easier for employees to find documents, people, or topics quickly, even if they weren't directly shared with them.

- **Example:** Searching for "Q3 Marketing Plan" can return results from a SharePoint document library, a Teams channel file, or even an email in Outlook.

Good to Know: Using consistent metadata and naming conventions improves search accuracy, making knowledge retrieval faster and more intuitive.

6. Security and Compliance Across Microsoft 365
SharePoint inherits the **security and compliance features** of Microsoft 365. This includes **conditional access, data loss prevention (DLP), retention policies, and encryption**. Teams and OneDrive also rely on SharePoint's backend for shared files, ensuring that security policies are consistently applied.

- **Example:** A law firm can control who accesses sensitive client contracts, enforce retention schedules, and track who viewed or modified a document—all while users collaborate in Teams or SharePoint.

Watch Out For: Always review permissions at the site, library, and document levels. Even with Microsoft 365 security, human error can lead to accidental data exposure.

7. Supporting Hybrid Work and Remote Collaboration
SharePoint, as part of Microsoft 365, supports **remote and hybrid work** seamlessly. Users can access documents, dashboards, and project sites from any device, anywhere. Coupled with Teams and OneDrive, SharePoint becomes the backbone for a connected, productive workforce.

- **Example:** An international team can update a product roadmap in SharePoint, host meetings in Teams, and share insights in a OneNote notebook—all in real-time, without worrying about version conflicts or lost emails.

Good to Know: Using SharePoint with Teams channels enhances engagement, as employees interact with content, chat, and updates all in one place.

8. Power BI and Analytics Integration
SharePoint can serve as a **data repository for Power BI dashboards**, allowing teams to visualize trends and metrics directly from shared documents and lists. This makes insights actionable and accessible across the organization.

- **Example:** A sales team can create a SharePoint list tracking client interactions and visualize it in Power BI to monitor performance, spot opportunities, and predict revenue trends.

Quick Tip: Use built-in templates and connectors to link SharePoint lists with Power BI without needing complex coding skills.

9. Real-World Scenarios of SharePoint in Microsoft 365

- **Marketing Teams:** Store campaign assets, collaborate on presentations, automate approvals, and track progress via SharePoint and Teams.
- **Finance Departments:** Manage budgets, co-author spreadsheets, and generate reports that feed into Power BI dashboards.
- **Human Resources:** Host employee portals, manage onboarding workflows, and store HR policies with controlled access.
- **IT Departments:** Provide a central repository for documentation, process guidelines, and automated ticket handling via Power Automate.
- **Education Institutions:** Maintain course materials, assignments, and collaborative projects that integrate with Teams and OneDrive.

Pro Shortcut: Start by creating dedicated SharePoint sites for each department or major project. Link them to Teams channels and document libraries to streamline collaboration.

Summary

SharePoint's role in Microsoft 365 is that of a **central hub, collaboration backbone, and knowledge manager**. By connecting seamlessly with Teams, OneDrive, Office apps, Power Automate, and Power BI, it enables organizations to:

- Collaborate in real-time across locations and devices.
- Automate workflows and streamline approvals.
- Maintain secure and compliant data access.
- Make informed decisions through integrated analytics.
- Enhance knowledge management and search capabilities.

Quick Tip: Treat SharePoint as the foundation of your Microsoft 365 environment. Invest in structured sites, libraries, and workflows to maximize efficiency and adoption across your organization.

1.5 Real-World Uses for Teams and Organizations

SharePoint isn't just a tech platform—it's a practical, real-world solution that transforms how teams and organizations operate. By providing a centralized hub for documents, communication, workflows, and collaboration, SharePoint supports a wide variety of use cases across industries, business sizes, and team structures. Understanding how teams can leverage SharePoint effectively helps you see its value beyond theory, making it easier to implement in everyday operations.

1. Document Management and Collaboration

At its core, SharePoint acts as a **centralized document management system**. Teams can store files in **document libraries**, categorize them with metadata, and track versions over time. This means multiple team members can **co-author files** simultaneously without worrying about overwriting each other's work. For example, a marketing team working on a campaign plan can collaborate in real-time on a single Word document, with comments, version history, and workflow approvals all integrated into the same platform. This reduces the endless back-and-forth emails and ensures that everyone has access to the most recent version of any document.

Quick Tip: Encourage team members to check out the **"Version History"** **feature**—it's like having a time machine for your documents, letting you restore previous edits if something goes wrong.

2. Project Management and Task Tracking

SharePoint is ideal for **managing projects**, whether simple or complex. Using **lists, calendars, and task management tools**, teams can track deadlines, assign responsibilities, and monitor progress. For instance, a product development team can create a project site with task lists for design, prototyping, testing, and launch phases. Each task can include due dates, assigned members, and progress updates, all visible to the team in one organized location. Integration with **Microsoft Planner and Teams** further enhances visibility, allowing real-time notifications and updates.

Good to Know: By centralizing tasks, SharePoint reduces the risk of missed deadlines and miscommunication. It's like having a shared whiteboard that everyone can see and update simultaneously.

3. Knowledge Management and Intranet Solutions

Many organizations use SharePoint as an **internal knowledge hub or intranet**. Departments can create **communication sites** to share announcements, policies, best practices, and training materials. For example, the HR department can maintain an employee onboarding portal with step-by-step guides, videos, and forms. Employees have a single place to find all relevant information without needing to search through email threads or different drives. SharePoint's **search and metadata features** make finding specific content fast and intuitive.

Quick Tip: Add **tags and categories** to documents and pages to help team members locate important information quickly—think of it as creating an organized library for your company's knowledge.

4. Automated Workflows and Process Optimization

SharePoint integrates seamlessly with **Power Automate**, allowing teams to automate repetitive tasks and approvals. For instance, when a team submits a purchase request, a workflow can automatically route it for manager approval, notify accounting, and archive the request in the proper folder—all without manual intervention. This reduces errors, saves time, and ensures processes are consistent. Teams in HR, finance, and operations can particularly benefit from automating approvals, document routing, and notifications.

Pro Shortcut: Start by automating one small workflow, like vacation requests or expense approvals. Once your team sees the benefits, scaling up to more complex processes becomes easier.

5. Compliance and Security Management

SharePoint offers **granular permission controls** that help organizations manage access to sensitive information. Teams can restrict documents, lists, or entire sites to specific users or groups. This is especially important in industries like healthcare, finance, or legal services, where compliance with regulations such as **HIPAA or GDPR** is critical. Audit logs and data retention policies help organizations track activity and maintain compliance. For example, a legal team can create a secure library for confidential contracts, ensuring that only authorized personnel can view or edit them.

Watch Out For: Always review and update permissions regularly—people change roles, and outdated access can pose a security risk.

6. Enterprise Collaboration Across Geographies

For organizations with **remote teams or multiple office locations**, SharePoint enables seamless collaboration. Employees in different regions can access the same documents, communicate updates, and participate in projects without needing to be physically present. For instance, a global consulting firm can maintain a central repository for client proposals, allowing consultants in New York, London, and Tokyo to contribute simultaneously. This eliminates time-zone barriers and reduces the friction of remote teamwork.

Good to Know: Combining SharePoint with **Microsoft Teams** makes real-time collaboration even easier, with chat, video calls, and shared file access in one integrated experience.

7. Industry-Specific Applications

Different industries have leveraged SharePoint in unique ways:

- **Education:** Schools and universities use SharePoint to host course materials, student assignments, and faculty collaboration portals. Teachers can track grades, share resources, and communicate with students, while administrators manage schedules and compliance documentation.

- **Healthcare:** Hospitals manage patient forms, staff schedules, and clinical guidelines. Secure document storage and access controls ensure sensitive data is protected.
- **Manufacturing:** Companies track production schedules, inventory lists, and safety procedures. Automated workflows reduce downtime and improve operational efficiency.
- **Retail:** Retail chains use SharePoint to distribute training manuals, promotional campaigns, and HR communications across multiple stores.

Quick Tip: Think creatively—SharePoint isn't just for files. Any process or knowledge management need can potentially be improved with sites, lists, and workflows.

8. Communication and Employee Engagement

Beyond project management and document storage, SharePoint can **enhance internal communication**. Using news pages, announcements, and discussion boards, companies keep employees informed and engaged. A department might post updates about new policies, celebrate team achievements, or share industry insights. Engagement features such as **likes, comments, and alerts** allow employees to participate actively rather than passively consuming information.

Pro Shortcut: Highlight key news on your team site homepage. Visual cues, banners, or quick links help important updates stand out.

9. Integration with Business Intelligence and Analytics

SharePoint can integrate with **Power BI** to create dashboards and reports that visualize business data directly on team sites. Sales teams can track metrics, finance teams can monitor budgets, and operations teams can follow production KPIs—all without leaving the SharePoint environment. This integration provides actionable insights at a glance, helping teams make data-driven decisions quickly.

Good to Know: You don't need to be a data expert. Pre-built templates and dashboards make it easy to display meaningful information for your team.

10. Supporting Remote Work and Digital Transformation

In today's hybrid work environment, SharePoint is a critical tool for **digital transformation**. Teams can work from anywhere, access files securely, and collaborate seamlessly. Organizations adopting SharePoint often see improvements in productivity, transparency, and operational efficiency. For remote teams, it reduces reliance on email, shared drives, and disconnected apps, creating a unified, flexible, and scalable platform.

Watch Out For: A successful deployment requires planning. Clear site structures, permissions policies, and user training are essential for adoption.

Summary of Benefits for Teams and Organizations

- **Centralized content storage:** Everyone knows where to find and store documents.
- **Enhanced collaboration:** Real-time editing and communication improve teamwork.
- **Automated workflows:** Reduces repetitive work and errors.
- **Knowledge management:** Searchable libraries and metadata make finding information easy.
- **Security and compliance:** Protect sensitive data with fine-grained permissions and policies.
- **Scalability:** Supports small teams to enterprise-wide operations.
- **Integration with Microsoft 365:** Keeps all your tools connected.
- **Employee engagement:** News, announcements, and collaboration foster participation.
- **Data-driven decisions:** Dashboards and analytics provide actionable insights.
- **Flexibility for remote work:** Accessible anywhere, anytime, on any device.

In essence, SharePoint is not just a storage tool—it's a **comprehensive collaboration and knowledge management platform** that empowers teams to work smarter, faster, and more efficiently. Whether you are managing documents, tracking projects, automating workflows, or creating interactive dashboards, SharePoint provides the structure, tools, and flexibility that modern teams and organizations need to thrive. **Quick Tip:** Start small with a pilot project site, explore its capabilities, and gradually expand its use. By doing so, your team will gain confidence and see tangible benefits quickly, paving the way for wider organizational adoption.

Chapter 2: Getting Started

2.1 System Requirements and Access Options

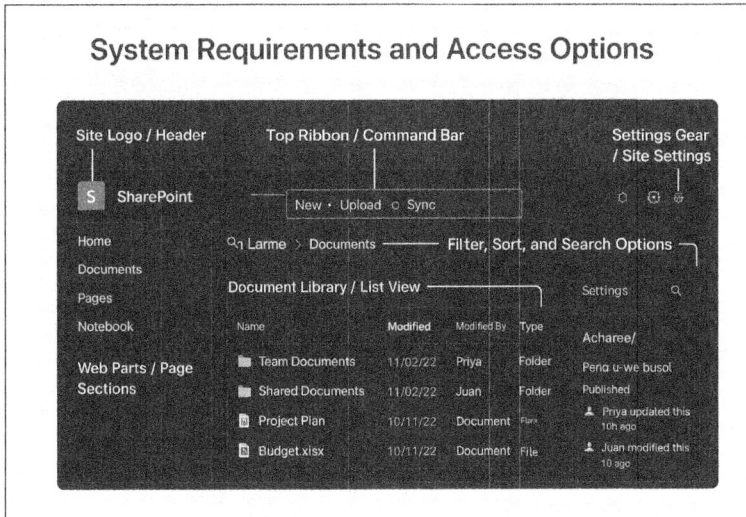

System Requirements and Access Options

Getting started with SharePoint might feel a little overwhelming at first, especially if this is your first time using a sophisticated collaboration platform. But don't worry—think of this chapter as your **friendly guide to preparing your system and understanding all the ways you can access SharePoint**. By the end, you'll feel confident that your computer, browser, or mobile device is ready, and you'll know exactly how to start using SharePoint effectively.

1. Understanding SharePoint Access Options

SharePoint comes in different forms and can be accessed in multiple ways. Knowing the differences is essential so you can pick the best method for your work style.

a. SharePoint Online (Cloud-Based)

This is the version included with **Microsoft 365 subscriptions**. It's hosted by Microsoft, meaning you don't have to worry about hardware, updates, or maintenance. Everything is accessible from your browser or mobile device.

- **Pros:**
  - ○ Accessible from anywhere with an internet connection
  - ○ Always up-to-date with the latest features
  - ○ Integrates seamlessly with Teams, OneDrive, and Office apps
- **Cons:**
  - ○ Requires an internet connection (though offline sync is possible with OneDrive)
  - ○ Subscription-based

    Quick Tip: Think of SharePoint Online like renting a fully furnished office—you just show up and start working.

b. SharePoint On-Premises (Server-Based)

Some organizations prefer to host SharePoint on their own servers. This is called **SharePoint Server** or **on-premises**. It offers more control but requires IT staff to manage servers, updates, and backups.

- **Pros:**
  - ○ Greater control over security and customization
  - ○ Useful for organizations with strict compliance requirements
- **Cons:**
  - ○ Requires significant IT resources
  - ○ Updates and upgrades can be slower

    Good to Know: Many organizations use a **hybrid approach**, combining both online and on-premises SharePoint for flexibility.

c. Mobile Access

SharePoint is fully mobile-friendly. You can download the **SharePoint mobile app** on iOS or Android, giving you access to sites, libraries, and news feeds on the go.

- **Example:** Imagine you're commuting and need to approve a document—you can do it right from your phone.

2. Minimum System Requirements

Before diving in, it's important to ensure your device meets the system requirements. SharePoint Online is designed to run on modern browsers and devices, but following these guidelines will give you a smooth experience.

a. Browser Requirements

SharePoint Online works best with modern browsers. While older browsers may still load SharePoint, you might encounter missing features or performance issues.

- **Recommended Browsers:**
  - Microsoft Edge (latest version) – best compatibility
  - Google Chrome (latest version)
  - Mozilla Firefox (latest version)
  - Safari (on macOS, latest version)
    Watch Out For: Avoid using Internet Explorer—it's no longer supported for SharePoint Online and may cause errors or missing features.

b. Operating Systems

SharePoint is compatible with a variety of operating systems:

- **Windows:** Windows 10 or later
- **Mac:** macOS 10.14 (Mojave) or later
- **Mobile:** iOS 13 or later, Android 8 or later
  Pro Shortcut: Keep your browser and operating system updated for the best performance and security.

c. Hardware Recommendations

While SharePoint is not resource-heavy, smoother performance is achieved with:

- At least **8 GB RAM** (16 GB preferred for heavy users)

- Modern multi-core processor (i5 or better recommended)
- Stable internet connection (at least 10 Mbps for large files or video content)

  Good to Know: If your device is older, you can still access SharePoint, but large libraries or high-resolution media may load slower.

3. Accessing SharePoint for the First Time

There are several ways you can start using SharePoint depending on your setup:

a. Through Microsoft 365 Portal

1. Open your browser and go to https://www.office.com
2. Sign in with your **work or school Microsoft account**
3. Click the **SharePoint icon** from the app launcher

b. Via Direct Site URL

Some organizations provide a direct URL to their SharePoint site. Enter it in your browser, sign in, and you're ready to go.

c. Using the SharePoint Mobile App

1. Download the app from **App Store** or **Google Play**
2. Sign in with your Microsoft 365 credentials
3. Access team sites, libraries, and news on the go

   Quick Tip: Bookmark your frequently used SharePoint sites for faster access.

4. Sign-In Options and Security

SharePoint uses **Microsoft 365 credentials** for access. Depending on your organization, additional security features may be enabled:

- **Multi-Factor Authentication (MFA):** Adds a layer of security by requiring a second verification step, like a text message or app notification.

- **Single Sign-On (SSO):** If your company uses SSO, signing in to SharePoint will automatically log you into other Microsoft 365 apps.
  Watch Out For: Always log out from public computers and never share your password. Even with SSO, you maintain control over sensitive data.

5. Preparing Your Device for SharePoint

Before diving in, take a few minutes to ensure your device is ready:

1. **Update Your Browser:** Always use the latest version for security and compatibility.
2. **Install Required Apps:** OneDrive is essential for offline file access. Teams enhances collaboration.
3. **Check Network Connectivity:** A stable internet connection ensures smooth file uploads and downloads.
4. **Set Permissions:** Ensure you have the correct access levels for the sites you need—owners, members, or visitors.
   Pro Shortcut: If using a personal device, consider enabling OneDrive sync to access files offline and keep them automatically updated.

6. Understanding Different Types of SharePoint Sites

When you access SharePoint, you'll encounter **different types of sites**:

- **Team Sites:** Designed for collaboration among team members. Includes document libraries, lists, and task trackers.
- **Communication Sites:** Best for broadcasting information across the organization, like newsletters or announcements.
- **Hub Sites:** Connects multiple sites under a shared navigation and branding. Ideal for departments or projects spanning multiple teams.
  Good to Know: Knowing which type of site you're accessing will help you understand where to store files, post updates, or collaborate effectively.

7. Quick Tips for Smooth Onboarding

- Bookmark your most frequently used SharePoint sites.
- Sync document libraries with OneDrive for offline access.
- Take a moment to explore the navigation menus—lists, libraries, and web parts are the building blocks.
- Don't worry if something seems confusing—most users take a few days to get fully comfortable.

8. Real-World Example: Getting Started in Action

Imagine you're joining the marketing team of a mid-sized company:

1. **Access the Site:** You receive a link to the team's SharePoint site.
2. **Sign In:** Use your Microsoft 365 credentials. MFA confirms it's you.
3. **Explore Libraries:** You find folders for campaign assets, presentations, and reports.
4. **Sync Files:** Click the OneDrive sync button to work on files offline.
5. **Check Notifications:** The homepage highlights recent updates and upcoming tasks.
6. **Integrate with Teams:** All files in the SharePoint document library automatically appear in your team's Teams channel.
   Within a few minutes, you are fully integrated into the workflow—without having to learn multiple platforms.

Summary

Getting started with SharePoint is about **preparing your device, understanding access options, and knowing the tools available**. Key takeaways include:

- Choose the right SharePoint version (Online or On-Premises) for your organization.
- Ensure your system meets browser, OS, and hardware requirements.
- Use Microsoft 365 credentials and enable MFA for security.
- Explore team sites, communication sites, and hub sites to understand where to collaborate.
- Integrate SharePoint with Teams, OneDrive, and Office apps for a seamless experience.

Quick Tip: Think of SharePoint as your **digital office**—once your desk (device) and tools (apps, browser, permissions) are set up, collaborating becomes effortless.

2.2 Navigating the SharePoint Interface

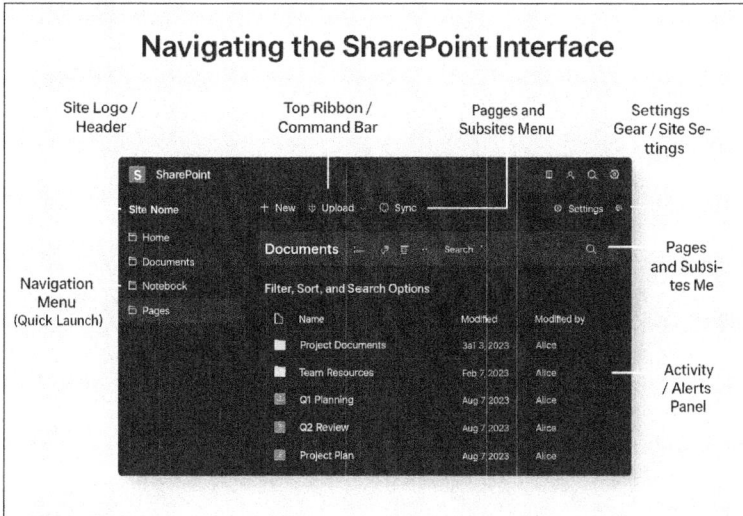

Navigating the SharePoint Interface

Navigating SharePoint for the first time can feel a bit like walking into a new office—you see all the rooms, desks, and tools, and it may feel overwhelming. But don't worry! Think of this as a friendly tour where we walk through every corner together, step by step, so you can confidently find what you need and start collaborating effectively. By the end of this section, you'll understand how SharePoint's interface is organized and how to move around like a pro.

Understanding the Home Page Layout
When you first open a SharePoint site, the **home page** is your central hub. It's designed to give you a quick overview of what's happening and easy access to the tools you need. At the top, you'll usually find the **site header**,

which contains the site name, logo, and navigation links. These links often include sections like **Documents, Pages, News, and Lists**. Think of these as the main hallways connecting you to different rooms in your digital office.

Below the header, you'll see **web parts**—blocks of content that show updates, announcements, documents, or calendars. Each web part is interactive, so you can click, open, or even edit items directly. This is similar to bulletin boards in a real office where important notices and documents are displayed.

Quick Tip: Hover over different web parts and links. Many of them reveal extra options, like opening menus, editing content, or sorting items. Don't be afraid to explore!

Left-Hand Navigation Panel

Most SharePoint sites include a **left-hand navigation panel**, also called the site menu. This is like the directory in a building, helping you quickly find rooms (libraries, lists, or pages) without wandering around. Common sections include: **Home, Documents, Site Contents, Pages, and Recent**. Clicking any link will take you directly to that section, and many items will expand to reveal sub-links for even more specific areas.

Good to Know: The navigation panel can sometimes be customized by your site owner. If you don't see a link you expect, check the top navigation or ask your SharePoint admin.

Top Navigation and Search Bar

Across the top, you'll often see a **search bar**. This is one of SharePoint's most powerful tools—it can search **documents, lists, pages, and even people** in your organization. Enter keywords, and SharePoint will return results organized by relevance. Think of it like asking a helpful office assistant who knows where everything is stored.

Next to the search bar, there may be quick access icons for **Microsoft 365 apps, your profile, and notifications**. Notifications alert you when someone shares a file, updates a page, or assigns a task. Paying attention to these will help you stay on top of collaboration.

Document Libraries and Lists

Documents and lists are core to SharePoint. Document libraries store files like Word, Excel, or PowerPoint documents, while lists can track information such as tasks, contacts, or inventory. Libraries and lists often include **columns**, filters, and views. Columns help organize data by type (e.g., Name, Date Modified, Status), and filters let you narrow down results quickly. Views allow you to see items in a **list view, grid view, or gallery view**, depending on your preference.

Pro Shortcut: Try switching between different views to see which one makes your work easiest. Grid view is great for managing lots of items, while gallery view is perfect for images or visual content.

Using the Command Bar

At the top of libraries and lists, you'll see the **command bar** with buttons like **New, Upload, Sync, Edit, and Share**. This is your toolkit for interacting with content.

- **New:** Create a new document, folder, or list item.
- **Upload:** Add files from your computer.
- **Sync:** Connect the library to OneDrive for offline access.
- **Edit:** Modify content directly in the browser.
- **Share:** Invite colleagues to view or edit items.

Quick Tip: Don't worry if you accidentally make a change—you can often **undo edits** or revert to previous versions using the **version history** feature.

Breadcrumb Navigation

SharePoint often uses **breadcrumb navigation** near the top of pages. This shows your path, like Home > Documents > Marketing > Campaign Files. Clicking any part of the breadcrumb takes you back to that section. Think of it as leaving a trail of breadcrumbs in a forest—you'll never get lost.

Customizing Your View

SharePoint allows you to **personalize your experience**. You can pin frequently used libraries or pages, adjust the layout of lists, and create **favorites** for quick access. These small adjustments make navigation much more efficient and tailored to your workflow.

Watch Out For: If a page looks different from the screenshots you see in guides, your organization may have customized the site. The layout might vary, but the core navigation principles remain the same.

Tips for Efficient Navigation

- Use the **search bar** first—it's faster than manually hunting for documents.
- **Pin important libraries** or lists to the left-hand navigation panel.
- Regularly check **recent documents** to quickly access files you've used.
- Learn the **keyboard shortcuts** for your browser and SharePoint; they can save a lot of time.
- Explore **mobile navigation** if you often work on the go; the SharePoint mobile app mirrors most desktop functionality.

Example in Practice: Imagine you are part of the HR team and need to update an onboarding checklist. First, go to the **Documents library** via the left-hand menu, search for "Onboarding Checklist" in the search bar, open the document, and edit directly in the browser. Once done, SharePoint automatically saves your changes, and your team sees the updated version instantly.

Summary

Navigating SharePoint is all about understanding its **home page layout, navigation panels, command bars, and document management features**. Remember, SharePoint is designed to be intuitive once you get familiar with it. Don't worry if it feels confusing at first—exploration is part of the learning process. Bookmark your most-used pages, use search effectively, and take advantage of OneDrive sync to make your experience seamless. **Quick Tip:** Think of SharePoint as your digital office—once you know the hallways, rooms, and tools, collaborating and finding information becomes natural and effortless.

2.3 Understanding Sites, Libraries, and Lists

SharePoint can feel like a big digital office building, and to navigate it effectively, you need to understand its main "rooms" and "storage areas." The key building blocks you'll interact with every day are **Sites, Libraries, and Lists**. Once you grasp how these work together, you'll move around SharePoint confidently and know exactly where to find and store your files and information.

Sites: The Digital Workspace

Think of a **SharePoint Site** as an entire office or department within a larger organization. Each site is a dedicated space for a team, project, or business function. For example, your marketing team might have a **Marketing Site**, the HR team a **HR Site**, and a project team a **Project Site**. Sites contain everything a team needs to collaborate: documents, pages, lists, news, calendars, and apps.

Good to Know: Sites can be **team sites** or **communication sites**. Team sites are designed for collaboration, where everyone can edit, share, and co-author content. Communication sites are more like bulletin boards, where information flows **from the top down**, ideal for company-wide announcements or resources.

Each site can be customized with **themes, navigation menus, and web parts** to suit the team's workflow. This means two sites may look different even within the same organization, but their core structure is similar.

Quick Tip: Think of sites as different departments in your digital office. Knowing which site to visit is your first step to finding the right documents or information.

Libraries: Organized File Storage

Within each site, you'll find **Document Libraries**—these are like filing cabinets in your office. Libraries store all your files: Word documents, Excel spreadsheets, PowerPoint presentations, PDFs, and more. They are designed to make file storage organized, searchable, and collaborative.

Key Features of Libraries:

- **Columns and Metadata:** Files can be tagged with categories, dates, owners, or project names. This helps you filter and sort documents quickly.
- **Views:** Choose how you see your files—**list view**, **grid view**, or **gallery view**. For images or visual content, gallery view is ideal, while grid or list views work best for large sets of files.
- **Version History:** SharePoint automatically keeps previous versions of files, so you can restore or compare changes if needed.
- **Check-In / Check-Out:** In team environments, checking out a document ensures that only you can edit it until you check it back in, preventing accidental overwrites.

Example in Practice: Imagine your team is working on a quarterly report. The **Marketing Documents Library** stores all drafts, spreadsheets, and graphics. By adding columns like "Owner" and "Status," you instantly see who is responsible for each file and which files are ready for review.

Lists: Structured Information Management

While libraries store files, **Lists** are like structured spreadsheets or databases for managing information. Lists can track tasks, contacts, inventory, events, or anything that requires structured data. Each item in a list has **columns**, such as "Title," "Due Date," "Status," or "Assigned To," making it easy to organize, filter, and sort data.

Common Uses for Lists:

- **Task Tracking:** Keep track of project tasks, deadlines, and responsibilities.
- **Event Management:** Organize meetings, deadlines, and company events.

- **Asset Tracking:** Manage equipment, software licenses, or inventory.
- **Issue Tracking:** Log bugs or problems and monitor their resolution.

Pro Shortcut: Lists can include **custom forms, conditional formatting, and automated flows** using Power Automate, so tasks like approvals or notifications happen automatically.

How Sites, Libraries, and Lists Work Together

Think of a site as your department's digital headquarters. Inside, libraries act as filing cabinets holding your documents, and lists act like structured spreadsheets tracking tasks, assets, or information. Together, they form a **complete ecosystem** for collaboration:

- A marketing team site may have a **Documents Library** for campaign materials and a **List** for tracking social media posts.
- An HR site could have a **Library** for employee handbooks and a **List** for onboarding tasks.
- A project site might include a **Library** for project files and a **List** for action items, deadlines, and assigned team members.

Quick Tip: Use the **Search Bar** to find content across sites, libraries, and lists. SharePoint's search function often surfaces results faster than manually browsing folders.

Customization and Permissions

SharePoint lets you **customize sites, libraries, and lists** to suit your workflow. You can adjust columns, views, forms, and web parts, giving each team exactly what they need. Permissions can also be set at the site, library, or list level, controlling who can **view, edit, or manage content**. This ensures that sensitive information is protected while keeping collaboration seamless.

Watch Out For: Over-customizing can make navigation confusing for new team members. Stick to clear, consistent naming conventions and logical layouts.

Example Scenario: Your team is preparing for a product launch. The **Launch Site** includes a **Library** for design files, a **List** for tasks with due dates and owners, and a **News Web Part** for announcements. Team members can access all relevant content from one place without having to search across emails or shared drives.

Summary

Understanding **Sites, Libraries, and Lists** is the foundation of SharePoint. Sites are your digital departments, libraries are your filing cabinets, and lists are your structured spreadsheets. When you know how these components work together, you can navigate efficiently, collaborate effectively, and keep your organization's information organized and accessible. **Good to Know:** Think of SharePoint as a well-organized office building—once you know which rooms hold the files and which tables track tasks, your workday becomes much smoother and more productive.

2.4 Permissions and Access Basics

Understanding permissions and access in SharePoint is like knowing who has keys to which rooms in a physical office. The right permissions ensure that your team can work efficiently without stumbling over restrictions, while also keeping sensitive information secure. SharePoint uses a **layered approach** to permissions, letting you control access at the **site, library, folder, document, and list levels**.

SharePoint Permission Levels

SharePoint offers a set of predefined permission levels that are easy to understand:

- **Full Control:** Users can do everything—create, edit, delete content, manage permissions, and configure settings. This is usually reserved for site owners or administrators.
- **Edit:** Users can add, modify, and delete items in libraries and lists. Perfect for team members actively collaborating on content.
- **Contribute:** Users can add and edit items but cannot delete major elements or manage site settings. A common level for general contributors.

- **Read:** Users can view content but cannot make any changes. This is ideal for stakeholders who need information without editing rights.
- **Limited Access:** A system-generated permission that allows access to specific content without exposing the entire site.

Good to Know: These levels can be customized to meet your organization's specific needs. For example, you could create a "Project Reviewer" level that allows read-only access to most documents but edit access to a particular list.

Inheritance vs. Unique Permissions

By default, **permissions in SharePoint are inherited**. This means a library, folder, or document typically inherits the permissions of the parent site. While this simplifies management, there are times when unique permissions are necessary:

- **Breaking Inheritance:** You can break inheritance to assign specific permissions for a particular library, folder, or document. For instance, a confidential HR folder may require access only for HR team members while the rest of the site remains open to others.
- **Granting Access:** You can give access to individuals, groups, or security-enabled Microsoft 365 groups. SharePoint also supports external sharing, allowing access to people outside your organization with proper authentication.

Quick Tip: Avoid giving individual permissions to too many items; instead, use **groups**. Groups are easier to manage and reduce the chance of accidental access errors.

Understanding SharePoint Groups

SharePoint groups are **collections of users** with the same permission level. Common groups include:

- **Owners:** Full control over the site.
- **Members:** Edit and contribute content.
- **Visitors:** Read-only access.

Groups simplify permission management. Instead of adjusting permissions for each user individually, you can add or remove users from a group. Everyone in the group automatically inherits the assigned permissions.

Best Practices for Assigning Permissions

1. **Follow the Principle of Least Privilege:** Give users only the access they need to do their job. This limits accidental changes or exposure of sensitive data.
2. **Use Groups Whenever Possible:** Managing a few groups is easier than managing hundreds of individual permissions.
3. **Document Custom Permissions:** If you create unique permissions, keep a record of what was changed, why, and who has access.
4. **Regularly Review Permissions:** Over time, team members change roles. Regularly auditing permissions ensures the right people have the right access.
5. **Communicate Clearly:** Let your team know who can access what. Confusion can lead to unnecessary support requests.

Example Scenario: Imagine your company is preparing for a confidential product launch. You have a **Launch Site** with three libraries: Marketing, Development, and HR. You assign:

- **Marketing Library:** Edit access to marketing team members, read-only for executives.
- **Development Library:** Edit access only to the development team.
- **HR Library:** Full control to HR managers, restricted read-only for others.

This ensures that everyone can work on what they need without risking accidental exposure of confidential information.

External Sharing
SharePoint also allows sharing with people **outside your organization**, such as contractors or clients. You can share files or entire sites with:

- **Guest Users:** Individuals invited via email. They need to sign in with a Microsoft account or a one-time passcode.
- **Anonymous Links:** A less secure method that allows anyone with the link to access the content. Use this cautiously and only when necessary.

Watch Out For: Sharing at the site level is more powerful but also more risky. Consider sharing at the document or folder level to minimize exposure.

Understanding Access Requests

Users who don't have permission to view or edit content can send an **access request**. Site owners receive a notification and can approve or deny the request. This feature is handy for teams that frequently onboard new members or collaborate with external partners.

Pro Shortcut: Configure automatic access request settings to streamline approvals. For example, you can designate a team lead to approve all requests instead of having site owners handle them individually.

Auditing and Monitoring Permissions

SharePoint provides tools to **audit who has accessed what**, which is essential for security and compliance. You can see:

- Who viewed or edited a document
- When permissions were changed
- Which users or groups have access to specific content

Regular audits help prevent security issues and ensure your organization remains compliant with internal and regulatory requirements.

Summary

Permissions and access control are critical for both collaboration and security in SharePoint. Sites, libraries, folders, documents, and lists all have layered permission options. Using **SharePoint groups, inheritance wisely, external sharing, and access requests** ensures a safe and efficient working environment. **Good to Know:** Treat permissions like keys in your office—only give people the keys they need and regularly check that no extra copies are floating around. By mastering permissions, you can confidently share and collaborate without compromising security.

2.5 Creating Your First Team Site

Creating your first SharePoint team site can feel like setting up a new office in the digital world. A well-structured site becomes the central hub for your team's documents, communications, and workflows. Don't worry if it feels overwhelming at first—this guide will walk you through every step in a friendly, clear, and supportive way. By the end, you'll have a fully functional team site ready for collaboration.

Step 1: Accessing SharePoint

Start by logging into your **Microsoft 365 account**. On the home dashboard, click the **SharePoint** icon. You'll land on the SharePoint start page, which displays all sites you're a member of. Think of this as your "lobby," where you can navigate to different rooms (sites) or set up a new one.

Quick Tip: Use a modern browser like Edge, Chrome, or Firefox for the best SharePoint experience.

Step 2: Choosing the Right Site Type

SharePoint offers two main site types for teams:

- **Team Site:** Ideal for collaboration within a group. Members can create, edit, and share documents, access shared calendars, and communicate via integrated Microsoft 365 tools.
- **Communication Site:** Best for broadcasting information to a wider audience. It's designed for news, announcements, and showcasing content rather than collaborative editing.

For your first site, we'll focus on a **Team Site**, which is perfect for everyday collaboration.

Step 3: Starting the Site Creation Process

1. Click **+ Create Site** at the top of the SharePoint home page.
2. Select **Team Site**.
3. Fill in the **Site Name** and **Site Description**:
   - **Site Name:** Choose something clear and recognizable (e.g., "Marketing Projects" or "Product Launch Team").
   - **Site Description:** Provide a brief overview of the site's purpose. This helps new members understand the site's focus.

Good to Know: SharePoint automatically generates a site email address based on the site name, which is useful for connecting with Microsoft Teams or sending alerts.

Step 4: Setting Privacy and Permissions
You'll be asked to choose the site's privacy:

- **Private:** Only members you invite can access the site. This is the safest option for confidential projects.
- **Public:** Anyone in your organization can access the site. Useful for broad collaboration or resource sharing.

Invite members by entering their **Microsoft 365 usernames or email addresses**. You can always add or remove members later.

Watch Out For: Avoid making sensitive project sites public. Privacy settings can be changed later, but it's best to start with the right level of security.

Step 5: Exploring the Team Site Layout
Once the site is created, SharePoint provides a default layout:

- **Home Page:** Serves as the main dashboard with news, quick links, and activity feeds.
- **Document Library:** Central place for storing and organizing files. Think of it as your digital filing cabinet.
- **Lists:** Used for tracking tasks, events, or other structured data.
- **Pages:** Additional customizable pages for content, instructions, or resources.

Quick Tip: Customize the home page to highlight the most important information for your team. For example, add a "Project Milestones" section or embed a team calendar.

Step 6: Adding and Organizing Content
Start adding content to your document libraries:

1. Click **Documents** in the left-hand menu.
2. Use **Upload** to add files or drag and drop from your computer.
3. Create folders to organize files logically (e.g., "Reports," "Presentations," "Meeting Notes").

Good to Know: SharePoint allows simultaneous collaboration on Office files. Multiple team members can edit Word, Excel, or PowerPoint documents at the same time without conflicts.

Step 7: Using Lists to Track Information
Lists are incredibly versatile:

- **Tasks List:** Track project tasks, assign owners, and set due dates.
- **Issue Tracker:** Manage project issues or bugs.
- **Custom Lists:** Define your own columns for any type of data.

Quick Tip: Use **views** to filter and sort list items. For example, show only tasks due this week or highlight items assigned to a specific team member.

Step 8: Integrating Microsoft 365 Tools
Your team site can seamlessly integrate with **Teams, Planner, and Outlook**:

- **Teams:** Connect your SharePoint site to a Microsoft Teams channel for real-time chat and file access.
- **Planner:** Add a Planner tab to track tasks visually using boards and charts.
- **Outlook:** Share calendars and events directly from the site.

Step 9: Customizing the Site Appearance
Make the site visually appealing and user-friendly:

- Change the **theme colors** to match your team's branding.
- Add **web parts** to the home page (e.g., Quick Links, News, Image Gallery).
- Rearrange sections to prioritize important content.

Pro Shortcut: Use templates from Microsoft 365 to quickly apply a professional layout without starting from scratch.

Step 10: Maintaining Your Team Site
A team site is most effective when actively maintained:

- Regularly review documents and remove outdated files.
- Update lists and tasks to reflect project progress.
- Encourage team members to engage with news posts and announcements.

Watch Out For: Avoid creating too many subfolders or pages—overcomplication can make navigation confusing. Keep the structure simple and intuitive.

Step 11: Best Practices for a Successful Team Site

- **Define clear roles:** Decide who can add content, edit, or approve documents.
- **Encourage collaboration:** Train team members to use co-authoring, commenting, and version history.
- **Regularly communicate updates:** Use announcements or news posts to keep everyone informed.
- **Leverage permissions wisely:** Only grant access as needed to protect sensitive data.
- **Audit usage:** Periodically review site activity to understand engagement and improve workflows.

Summary
Creating your first SharePoint team site sets the foundation for smooth collaboration, document management, and team communication. By following these steps—from choosing the site type and setting permissions

to organizing content and integrating Microsoft 365 tools—you can build a secure, functional, and engaging workspace. Remember, think of your team site like a digital office: clear organization, the right access, and active engagement are key to productivity. Don't worry if it feels complex at first—most users find that with a little exploration and consistent use, SharePoint becomes an indispensable tool for teamwork.

Chapter 3: Building and Customizing Sites

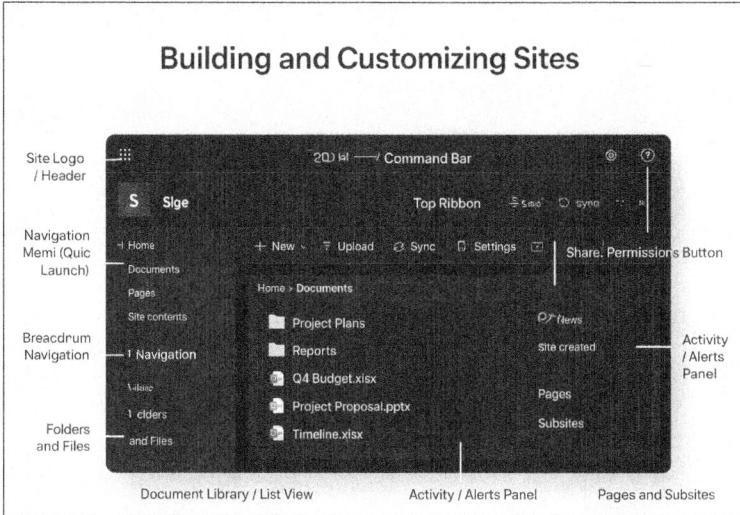

Building and Customizing Sites

3.1 Choosing Site Templates

 Choosing the right site template in SharePoint is like picking the blueprint for a building before construction begins. The template sets the foundation, structure, and functionality of your site, making it easier to create a site that fits your team's or organization's needs. With SharePoint, templates are designed to simplify setup, reduce manual configuration, and ensure best practices for collaboration and content management. In this section, we'll explore the different types of templates, how to choose the best one, and provide step-by-step guidance, all in a friendly, clear, and supportive tone. By the end, even beginners and non-tech-savvy users will feel confident in selecting the perfect template.

Understanding SharePoint Site Templates

A SharePoint site template is a pre-configured design that includes layouts, lists, libraries, and often, web parts. Think of it as a "starter kit" that gives you a head start rather than building everything from scratch. Each template has a purpose, whether it's for team collaboration, communication, project management, or departmental organization.

Templates in SharePoint can be broadly categorized into:

- **Team Site Templates:** Designed for collaboration within a specific group or department. Ideal for managing projects, storing documents, and coordinating tasks.
- **Communication Site Templates:** Focused on broadcasting information to a wider audience, such as company announcements, newsletters, or training materials.
- **Department-Specific Templates:** Pre-built for HR, Marketing, IT, or Finance departments with industry-specific content structures.
- **Custom Templates:** Created by your organization to meet unique requirements, often reflecting corporate branding and specific workflows.

Quick Tip: If you're unsure which template to choose, start with a team site for internal collaboration. You can always create additional sites for communication or other purposes later.

Step 1: Accessing Site Templates

1. Log in to your **Microsoft 365 account** and navigate to **SharePoint**.
2. Click + **Create Site** on the SharePoint homepage.
3. You will see options for **Team Site** and **Communication Site**. Some organizations may also display custom or department-specific templates here.

Watch Out For: If your organization has strict policies, some templates may be restricted or unavailable. Check with your IT administrator if you don't see all template options.

Step 2: Exploring Team Site Templates

Team site templates are your go-to choice for day-to-day collaboration. They usually include:

- **Document Libraries:** Ready-made folders for storing and organizing files.
- **Lists:** Task trackers, issue logs, and event schedules preconfigured for immediate use.
- **News Sections:** To post updates and announcements for your team.
- **Quick Links:** Easy navigation to important resources or external applications.

Examples of specialized team templates:

- **Project Management Template:** Includes a project task list, timeline, document library, and status reports.
- **HR Onboarding Template:** Contains document libraries for policies, forms, and training schedules.
- **Marketing Campaign Template:** Pre-built content calendars, asset libraries, and campaign tracking lists.

Good to Know: Each template can be customized further, so even if the default layout isn't perfect, you can modify it without losing the built-in structure.

Step 3: Exploring Communication Site Templates

Communication sites are designed to share information widely and keep your organization informed. Typical features include:

- **News and Announcements:** Highlight key updates, events, or organizational messages.
- **Hero Web Parts:** Large visual sections for important content or links.
- **Quick Links and Callouts:** Direct users to resources, policies, or training materials.
- **Event Calendars:** Centralized schedules for workshops, meetings, or launches.

Communication site templates often include:

- **Topic Template:** Organize content around a theme or subject.
- **Showcase Template:** Visually display products, services, or achievements.
- **Blank Template:** Start from scratch, ideal if you have a very specific layout in mind.

Step 4: Evaluating Which Template Fits Your Needs
When deciding on a template, consider the following factors:

- **Purpose of the Site:** Are you collaborating with a team, or sharing information broadly?
- **Audience:** Who will use the site? Internal team members, the whole organization, or external stakeholders?
- **Content Type:** Will the site host documents, lists, news posts, media, or a combination?
- **Future Expansion:** Will you need to add additional functionality later, such as workflows, automations, or integrations?

Pro Shortcut: Map out your site's goals on paper before selecting a template. For example, list all the content types, collaboration tools, and reporting needs. This helps ensure the chosen template aligns with your objectives.

Step 5: Creating a Site Using a Template

1. Click on the template that matches your purpose (Team Site or Communication Site).
2. Enter the **Site Name** and **Description**. Keep names clear, concise, and easy for team members to recognize.
3. Set **Privacy Settings** (Private or Public) depending on the intended audience.
4. Add **members** and assign **owners**. Remember, owners have full control, while members can contribute content.
5. Click **Finish** to create your site.

Your new site will now appear in the SharePoint homepage, ready for customization.

Step 6: Customizing Your Site Post-Template Selection

Templates provide a starting point, but customization allows you to tailor the site to your exact needs:

- **Web Parts:** Add news feeds, calendars, quick links, or image galleries.
- **Document Libraries:** Rename folders, add metadata, and set versioning policies.
- **Lists:** Customize columns, create views, and set up filters to manage tasks efficiently.
- **Pages:** Add new pages for project plans, departmental resources, or event guides.

Quick Tip: Don't be afraid to experiment. SharePoint allows you to move, edit, and remove components without breaking the site.

Step 7: Branding and Visual Identity

Templates may come with default themes, but adding your own branding improves recognition and engagement:

- Apply your organization's colors and logo.
- Customize the homepage banner or hero web part with images relevant to your team.
- Use consistent naming conventions for pages, libraries, and lists.

Watch Out For: Avoid overloading your homepage with too many visuals or web parts. A clean, simple layout improves usability and reduces confusion.

Step 8: Governance and Best Practices

Even with the perfect template, ongoing governance ensures the site remains organized and useful:

- **Define Roles:** Clearly assign owners, contributors, and viewers.

- **Establish Content Guidelines:** Provide instructions on naming files, updating lists, and posting news.
- **Monitor Usage:** Use site analytics to see which sections are used most and adjust content accordingly.
- **Regular Maintenance:** Archive outdated documents, remove unused web parts, and keep the structure simple.

Good to Know: SharePoint provides version history for all documents. Even if a file is edited or deleted, you can restore it to a previous version—like a "time machine" for your work.

Step 9: Leveraging Templates for Future Sites

Once you've customized a site, you can **save it as a template** to replicate its structure for future projects or teams. This is especially helpful for recurring project types or departmental workflows. Saved templates can include:

- Page layouts and web parts
- Lists and libraries
- Navigation structure
- Branding elements

Pro Shortcut: Use templates as a foundation for consistent site design across your organization, ensuring all teams follow best practices and can collaborate seamlessly.

Summary

Choosing the right SharePoint template is a crucial first step in building an organized, efficient, and visually appealing site. By understanding the differences between team sites, communication sites, and custom templates, evaluating your needs, and following best practices, you can select and customize a template that maximizes collaboration and productivity. Remember, templates are just starting points—SharePoint's flexibility allows you to tweak, enhance, and expand your site as your team's needs evolve. Treat your site like a dynamic workspace: start with a solid foundation, build with care, and continually adapt to support your team's goals. With patience and exploration, you'll soon find SharePoint becoming an indispensable hub for teamwork, information sharing, and productivity.

3.2 Designing Pages with Web Parts

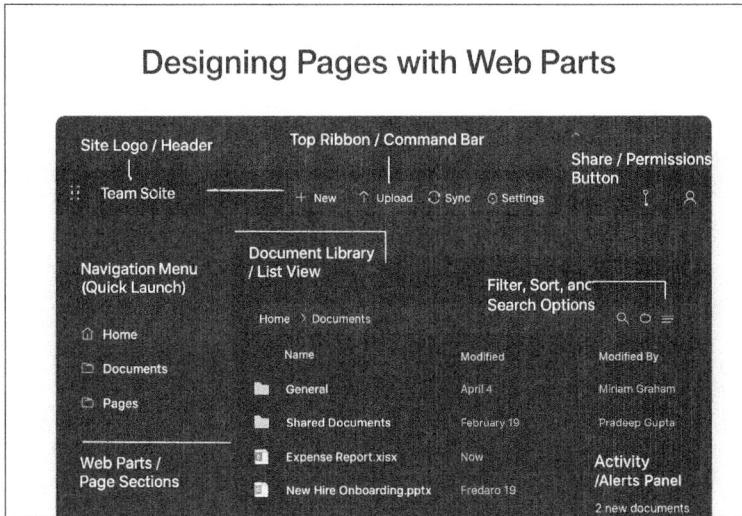

Designing pages with web parts in SharePoint is like assembling a digital workspace with modular building blocks. Each web part adds a piece of functionality or content, allowing you to craft pages that are both visually appealing and highly functional. This section will take you step by step through the concepts, best practices, and techniques for designing pages using web parts. Even beginners and non-tech-savvy users will feel comfortable building professional-looking pages by the end of this guide.

Understanding Web Parts

A web part is essentially a widget or component you can add to a SharePoint page to display content, functionality, or interactive elements. Think of it as a LEGO piece—you can arrange, stack, or customize each block to build a page that suits your needs. Web parts can display documents, lists, images, videos, calendars, news feeds, links, and more.

Types of Common Web Parts

- **Text Web Part:** For adding headings, paragraphs, or formatted text content. Perfect for introducing sections, sharing announcements, or providing instructions.
- **Image Web Part:** Adds single images or galleries. Ideal for visual storytelling, showcasing products, or illustrating instructions.
- **Document Library Web Part:** Displays a collection of files or folders, allowing users to access documents directly from the page.
- **List Web Part:** Shows tasks, contacts, or issue logs in an interactive, filterable list.
- **Quick Links Web Part:** Provides buttons or links to important pages, external sites, or resources for fast navigation.
- **News Web Part:** Displays news posts or announcements dynamically, helping teams stay informed.
- **Embed Web Part:** Allows embedding external content, such as videos, Power BI dashboards, or third-party apps.
- **Event Web Part:** Displays upcoming events, calendars, or team schedules.

Quick Tip: Start simple. Begin with 2–3 essential web parts to avoid overwhelming users. You can always add more as your page grows.

Step 1: Creating a Page

1. Navigate to your SharePoint site.
2. Click **New > Page** to create a modern page.
3. Choose a **layout template**—this determines how many sections and columns your page will have. Templates include one-column, two-column, three-column, or flexible sections.
4. Give your page a **title** that clearly communicates its purpose.

Watch Out For: Avoid vague titles like "Page 1" or "Info." A descriptive title helps team members quickly identify content.

Step 2: Adding Sections and Columns

Sections define horizontal blocks on your page, while columns divide those sections vertically. You can mix and match:

- **One-column section:** Ideal for focus content like announcements or a hero image.
- **Two-column section:** Useful for side-by-side text and images or document libraries next to instructions.
- **Three-column section:** Great for dashboards, multiple quick links, or summary panels.
- **Vertical sections:** Allows tall elements like navigation menus or large media components.

Pro Shortcut: Use consistent layouts across pages for a cohesive, professional look.

Step 3: Inserting Web Parts

1. Hover over a section, and click the + icon to add a web part.
2. Choose from the list of available web parts. You can search by name if you have many options.
3. Configure the web part properties. For example, when adding an image web part, you can choose alignment, add alt text for accessibility, and link the image to a page or document.

Step 4: Customizing Web Parts

Customization is key to making web parts functional and visually appealing:

- **Text Web Part:** Use headings (H1, H2, H3), bullets, bold, italics, and hyperlinks. Keep paragraphs concise and scannable.
- **Image Web Part:** Optimize images for web by resizing and compressing them. Use captions to provide context.
- **Document Library/List Web Part:** Configure default views, add filters, and enable sorting to help users find content quickly.
- **Quick Links Web Part:** Use descriptive text for links, organize them logically, and consider using buttons for high-priority actions.

Good to Know: Alt text for images is not just for accessibility—it also helps search within SharePoint.

Step 5: Arranging and Reordering Web Parts

Drag and drop web parts to rearrange them within sections or between sections. This allows you to prioritize content visually, placing the most important elements near the top.

Watch Out For: Too many web parts in a single section can slow page loading times. Aim for clarity and focus.

Step 6: Using Advanced Web Part Features

Some web parts have advanced options:

- **Dynamic Content:** The news web part can automatically pull the latest posts from a selected site or department.
- **Filters and Connections:** List web parts can connect to other web parts to display filtered data dynamically. For example, clicking a project name in one list could update tasks displayed in another web part.
- **Audience Targeting:** Display certain web parts only to specific groups, useful for HR announcements or department-specific content.

Pro Shortcut: Experiment with web part connections and filters in a test page first to see how interactions work before publishing.

Step 7: Previewing and Publishing Your Page

1. Click **Preview** to see how your page looks on desktop, tablet, and mobile views.
2. Check for readability, alignment, and visual balance.
3. Make adjustments as needed.
4. Click **Publish** when you're ready to share the page with your team or organization.

Quick Tip: Regularly update your pages to keep content fresh. SharePoint will maintain version history, so previous versions are always recoverable.

Step 8: Best Practices for Web Part Design

- **Consistency:** Use the same fonts, colors, and layouts across pages.
- **Clarity:** Avoid clutter; focus on essential content and functionality.
- **Accessibility:** Use alt text, headings, and sufficient contrast.
- **Navigation:** Use quick links, buttons, and menus to help users navigate efficiently.
- **Interactivity:** Where appropriate, add embedded media, links, or dynamic lists to keep users engaged.

Watch Out For: Avoid overusing animations or embedded videos that may distract from the primary content or slow down page loading.

Step 9: Leveraging Templates and Reusable Web Parts
Once you've created a well-designed page, you can save it as a **template** or reuse web parts across multiple pages. This ensures consistency and saves time when building additional pages.

Good to Know: SharePoint modern pages support **copying sections** between pages. If you have a standard layout with a text block, image, and document library, you can replicate it without recreating from scratch.

Step 10: Continuous Improvement and Feedback
After publishing, gather feedback from users. Monitor engagement through built-in analytics to see which web parts are most used and which may need improvement. Regularly update content and layouts to reflect evolving team needs and maintain relevance.

Summary
Designing pages with web parts in SharePoint gives you immense flexibility to create functional, attractive, and user-friendly pages. By understanding the types of web parts, carefully planning sections and layouts, customizing content, and following best practices, you can design pages that engage your audience and enhance collaboration. Remember, start simple, experiment, and build gradually. With patience and practice, web part design will become intuitive, allowing even beginners and non-tech-savvy users to create professional-quality SharePoint pages with confidence.

3.3 Branding and Layout Options

Branding and layout options in SharePoint allow you to give your site a unique look and feel while ensuring it's functional and user-friendly. Think of it as decorating your office: the right colors, logos, and layout make the space inviting, help people find what they need quickly, and reinforce your organization's identity. In this section, we'll cover how to customize branding and layouts in detail, with practical guidance suitable for beginners, seniors, and non-tech-savvy users.

Understanding Branding in SharePoint

Branding is more than just adding a logo or changing colors. It's about creating a consistent visual identity across your SharePoint environment so users instantly recognize your team, department, or organization. Good branding improves navigation, engagement, and overall usability.

Core Branding Elements:

- **Site Logo:** A visual identifier for your site, usually displayed in the top-left corner. It appears on pages, search results, and navigation menus.
- **Theme Colors:** Choose colors that match your organization's branding or create a palette that makes content readable and visually appealing.
- **Fonts and Typography:** While SharePoint has default fonts, you can choose typography that aligns with your organization's style. Headings, body text, and links should be consistent across pages.
- **Header Layout:** SharePoint modern pages offer several header layouts: standard, minimal, or compact. The header affects how your site looks and how much vertical space is used for navigation.

Step 1: Setting a Site Logo

1. Navigate to your SharePoint site.
2. Click the **Settings gear icon** in the top-right corner, then select **Site Information**.

3. Click **Change** next to the logo option and upload your organization's logo (PNG or SVG recommended).
4. Adjust the size if necessary and click **Save**.

Quick Tip: Use a transparent background for your logo. This ensures it looks good across different header colors.

Step 2: Applying a Theme

1. Go to **Settings** > **Change the look** > **Theme**.
2. Browse available SharePoint themes or create a custom theme.
3. Customize primary colors, accents, and text colors.
4. Preview the theme to ensure readability and aesthetics.
5. Click **Save** to apply the theme to your site.

Watch Out For: Avoid overly bright or clashing colors that make text hard to read. Accessibility is key.

Step 3: Customizing the Header Layout

- **Standard Header:** Includes logo and site name prominently; ideal for general-purpose team or department sites.
- **Compact Header:** Reduces header height; useful for dashboards or content-heavy sites.
- **Minimal Header:** Shows only essential elements; great for simple project sites or intranet pages.

Pro Shortcut: Keep headers consistent across pages for a professional look and easier navigation.

Step 4: Adjusting Navigation Layouts
Navigation is a critical part of site usability. SharePoint offers:

- **Top Navigation Bar:** Shows horizontal links across the top. Best for global navigation or smaller link sets.
- **Left-Hand Navigation (Quick Launch):** Vertical menu on the left side; ideal for department or project pages with many links.

- **Hub Navigation:** If your site is part of a hub, it can inherit hub navigation for consistency across related sites.

Step 5: Using Page Layouts and Sections
Page layout determines how content is organized and displayed. Consider:

- **Full-width sections:** Best for hero images or banners.
- **Multiple columns:** Useful for displaying text, images, and web parts side by side.
- **Vertical sections:** Allow tall elements like lists, embedded media, or forms.

Step 6: Customizing Footers
Footers are often overlooked but can reinforce branding and provide essential information:

- Add your organization's contact info, disclaimers, or links to policies.
- Use consistent colors and typography that match your header and overall theme.

Step 7: Accessibility Considerations
Good branding and layout also mean making your site accessible:

- Ensure sufficient color contrast between text and background.
- Use headings in a logical order (H1, H2, H3) for screen readers.
- Provide alt text for all images and web parts.

Good to Know: SharePoint modern pages automatically adjust layouts for mobile and tablet views, but always preview your design on different devices.

Step 8: Advanced Branding Options

- **Custom CSS (SharePoint Framework):** For advanced users or developers, custom CSS can adjust styles beyond the default options.
- **Theme Designer Tools:** Tools like the SharePoint Online Theme Designer let you generate and apply custom themes without coding.

- **Branding Packages:** Larger organizations may package fonts, colors, and logos for use across multiple sites.

Step 9: Maintaining Branding Consistency

- Create a **style guide** that outlines colors, fonts, logo usage, and layout preferences.
- Use **templates** for new pages to ensure a uniform look.
- Regularly review pages to maintain consistency and update branding elements as needed.

Step 10: Tips for Effective Page Layouts

- Keep content above the fold (visible without scrolling) for important announcements or key information.
- Use white space strategically to avoid clutter.
- Group related web parts together for easier navigation.
- Highlight high-priority content using banners, hero web parts, or emphasized text.

Quick Tip: Think of your page like a magazine layout: each section should have a clear purpose and flow naturally to the next.

Step 11: Testing and Feedback
Before finalizing your branding and layout:

- Preview your pages in **desktop, tablet, and mobile** views.
- Ask team members to navigate the site and provide feedback.
- Adjust colors, web part placement, and navigation based on real user input.

Summary
Branding and layout in SharePoint aren't just about looking good—they enhance usability, accessibility, and team identity. By carefully selecting logos, themes, headers, navigation, and layouts, you can create sites that are visually cohesive, easy to navigate, and welcoming for all users. Remember, consistency is key, accessibility is essential, and starting simple

while iterating based on feedback ensures your SharePoint site grows into a professional and user-friendly hub.

3.4 Managing Navigation and Site Settings

Managing navigation and site settings in SharePoint is a crucial step in creating a user-friendly, organized, and professional-looking site. Navigation ensures that your team members or organization can quickly find what they need without frustration, while proper site settings help maintain structure, permissions, and overall efficiency. Think of it like organizing a library: books (or content) need clear labels, well-defined sections, and a catalog system that anyone can use. In this section, we'll walk you through everything in detail, step by step, in a friendly, supportive tone that makes even beginners feel confident.

Understanding SharePoint Navigation

Navigation in SharePoint refers to the menus, links, and pathways that users take to access pages, libraries, lists, and content. SharePoint offers multiple navigation layers:

- **Top Navigation (Global Navigation):** A horizontal menu at the top of your site, ideal for key site areas or cross-site links.
- **Left-Hand Navigation (Quick Launch):** A vertical menu on the left side, perfect for department-specific pages, document libraries, or frequently used tools.
- **Hub Navigation:** If your site is part of a SharePoint hub, it can adopt a hub-wide menu to maintain consistency across related sites.

Step 1: Editing the Left-Hand Quick Launch Navigation

1. Click the **Settings gear icon** in the top-right corner of your site.
2. Select **Site Settings > Quick Launch** (or in modern pages, **Change the look > Navigation**).
3. To **add a new link**, click + **Add link**, provide a name and URL, and choose its position in the menu.
4. To **reorder links**, drag and drop them into the desired sequence.

5. To **edit or remove a link**, click the three dots next to the link and select the appropriate option.

Quick Tip: Group related links under headings to make the menu less cluttered and easier to scan. For example, group all document libraries under a "Documents" heading.

Step 2: Configuring Top Navigation

- Navigate to **Settings > Change the look > Navigation**.
- Add links to important pages, sites, or external resources that team members frequently use.
- You can also create **flyout menus** for multi-level navigation, which is especially helpful for larger organizations with complex site structures.

Watch Out For: Avoid overly long top navigation menus. If there are too many items, users might get overwhelmed. Consider submenus for organization.

Step 3: Using Hub Navigation (If Applicable)

1. If your site is associated with a hub, hub navigation can be activated automatically.
2. Links and site branding from the hub will display at the top of your site.
3. This is particularly useful for maintaining **branding consistency** across multiple team or department sites.

Pro Shortcut: Hub navigation is ideal for larger organizations. Even if your site isn't part of a hub, you can simulate hub-like menus using consistent top navigation across your sites.

Step 4: Understanding Site Settings

Site settings allow you to control the structure, permissions, and functionality of your SharePoint site. Key areas include:

- **Site Permissions:** Manage who can view, edit, or administer your site. Proper permissions prevent accidental deletions or unwanted changes.
- **Site Information:** Update the site name, description, logo, and privacy settings.
- **Regional Settings:** Configure time zones, locale, and language to ensure content is accurate and accessible for all team members.
- **Search Settings:** Customize how users search for content within your site, including metadata and search scopes.

Step 5: Adjusting Site Permissions

1. Go to **Settings > Site Permissions**.
2. Choose **Members**, **Owners**, or **Visitors** to assign roles.
3. To add someone new, click **Invite People** and enter their email addresses.
4. Consider using **SharePoint Groups** to simplify permission management for larger teams.

Quick Tip: Always follow the principle of least privilege—give users only the access they need. This reduces errors and protects sensitive data.

Step 6: Configuring Site Libraries and Lists

Navigation is closely tied to libraries and lists. Make sure your document libraries, calendars, or task lists are easy to find from your menus.

- **Link libraries to Quick Launch:** Click the library > **Settings > Navigation**, then select "Show in Quick Launch."
- **Use headings for clarity:** For example, group all project-related libraries under a "Project Docs" heading.
- **Consider folder structures carefully:** Too many nested folders can make navigation confusing. Use metadata tagging where possible.

Step 7: Customizing Pages for Navigation

- Use **web parts** like **Quick Links** to create visually appealing navigation panels.

- Highlight important pages or tools using **Hero web parts** or **Call to Action buttons**.
- Ensure that navigation panels are **consistent across pages** to reduce confusion.

Good to Know: SharePoint modern pages automatically adjust navigation for mobile and tablet views, but it's always a good idea to **preview** how your navigation looks on different devices.

Step 8: Testing Navigation and Site Settings
Before finalizing your structure:

- Ask team members to navigate the site and provide feedback.
- Test links to ensure they point to the correct pages or documents.
- Verify permissions by logging in as a standard user to see what is visible.

Step 9: Maintaining Navigation Over Time

- Regularly review Quick Launch and top menus to remove outdated links.
- Update headings and link names as projects evolve or team responsibilities change.
- Consider creating a **navigation guide** for team members to explain the menu structure and where content is located.

Step 10: Tips for Effective Navigation Design

- Keep the menu simple and intuitive—avoid too many sub-levels.
- Use **clear, descriptive names** for links and headings.
- Leverage **visual elements** like icons or highlighted links for critical tools.
- Group related content logically (e.g., all HR resources under one heading).

Quick Tip: Think of your SharePoint site like a map. Users should be able to reach their destination (document, page, or tool) in no more than 3 clicks.

Summary

Managing navigation and site settings effectively ensures that your SharePoint site is easy to use, well-organized, and aligned with your team or organization's needs. By carefully planning menus, links, permissions, and page structures, you create an intuitive environment where users can quickly find the content they need. Regular testing, feedback, and updates will keep the site efficient, user-friendly, and adaptable to changes over time.

3.5 Best Practices for Site Structure

Creating a well-structured SharePoint site is like building a well-organized home: everything should have its place, be easy to find, and work smoothly for the people using it. A clear, logical site structure improves productivity, reduces confusion, and ensures that team members or stakeholders can access information quickly and efficiently. In this section, we'll go through detailed, step-by-step guidance, practical examples, and helpful tips to make your site easy to navigate and manage.

Understanding the Importance of Site Structure

A good site structure acts as the backbone of your SharePoint environment. Without it, users may struggle to find content, documents could be misplaced, and workflows might be disrupted. Key benefits of a strong site structure include:

- **Improved usability:** Users can quickly locate the information they need.
- **Efficient collaboration:** Teams can share, edit, and manage content seamlessly.
- **Scalability:** The site can grow with your organization without becoming cluttered.
- **Better governance:** Easier to manage permissions, compliance, and data retention.

Step 1: Plan Before You Build

Before creating pages, libraries, and lists, spend time planning:

- **Identify the purpose of the site:** Is it for a department, project, or organization-wide collaboration?
- **Determine key content areas:** Think about the main categories or functions the site needs to serve (e.g., Projects, HR Resources, Reports).
- **Consider user roles:** Who will access the site, and what content will they need?

Quick Tip: Sketch a simple **site map** on paper or use digital tools like PowerPoint or Lucidchart. This visual blueprint will help you plan menus, libraries, and pages logically.

Step 2: Define Sites, Subsites, and Pages
SharePoint allows you to organize content into:

- **Sites:** High-level containers for a department, project, or topic.
- **Subsites:** Optional, smaller areas under a main site for focused projects or teams. Modern SharePoint often favors a flat structure with hub sites rather than multiple subsites.
- **Pages:** Individual content areas such as a project dashboard, announcements page, or policy library.

Good to Know: A flat structure is generally easier to maintain and scale than a deeply nested one. Consider using **hub sites** to group related sites instead of creating multiple layers of subsites.

Step 3: Organize Libraries and Lists
Document libraries and lists are where your content lives. Follow these guidelines:

- **Use descriptive names:** Name libraries clearly, e.g., "Project Documents – Q4 2025" rather than just "Documents."
- **Group related content:** For example, all HR forms can be under a single "HR Resources" library with folders for Policies, Templates, and Reports.

- **Minimize folders where possible:** Instead of deep folder hierarchies, use **metadata tags** for filtering and searching content efficiently.

Pro Shortcut: Metadata allows users to filter, sort, and group documents dynamically without having to dig through folders. Tags like "Project Name," "Department," or "Document Type" can save time.

Step 4: Plan Navigation Around Content
Navigation should reflect the structure of your site. Tips include:

- **Quick Launch (Left Menu):** Use for frequently accessed libraries, lists, or pages.
- **Top Navigation:** Link to main sites, hubs, or critical pages.
- **Consistency:** Keep link names, ordering, and headings consistent across all pages.

Watch Out For: Avoid overwhelming users with too many navigation links. Too many options can create decision fatigue. Group similar items and use headings.

Step 5: Consider Permissions and Access
Good structure goes hand-in-hand with proper access control:

- **Assign permissions at the right level:** Prefer library- or folder-level permissions over individual documents.
- **Use SharePoint Groups:** Create groups like Owners, Members, and Visitors for easier management.
- **Document sensitivity:** For confidential documents, create a dedicated library with restricted access.

Quick Tip: Use the principle of least privilege—give users the minimum access they need to perform their tasks.

Step 6: Plan for Search and Discoverability
Even with perfect navigation, users may rely on search. To improve discoverability:

- **Use clear titles and headings** in documents and pages.
- **Add metadata and tags** for better search results.
- **Organize content logically** so users understand where to look first.

Step 7: Establish a Governance Model

A governance model ensures that your site remains organized and functional over time:

- **Content ownership:** Assign responsible users for each library or page.
- **Review schedules:** Regularly check for outdated or unused content.
- **Standards and naming conventions:** Document these to maintain consistency across the site.

Pro Shortcut: Create a simple **site governance checklist** including tasks like reviewing permissions, updating links, and cleaning up old documents.

Step 8: Design for Scalability

Your site should grow with your team:

- Avoid overly complex structures that become difficult to maintain.
- Use hub sites to connect multiple related sites.
- Leverage templates for new pages or sites to maintain consistency.

Step 9: Use Visual Elements to Enhance Structure

- **Web Parts:** Use Quick Links, Hero, or Highlighted Content web parts to make important content easy to find.
- **Icons and images:** Visual cues help users quickly identify sections.
- **Consistency in branding:** Colors, fonts, and layouts make navigation intuitive.

Step 10: Test and Iterate

- Ask team members to navigate your site and provide feedback.

- Make adjustments to menus, library structures, and page layouts based on usage patterns.
- Monitor how users search and interact with content to identify pain points.

Good to Know: SharePoint modern pages allow live adjustments and previews, so you can make improvements without disrupting users.

Summary

Following best practices for site structure ensures your SharePoint environment is intuitive, efficient, and scalable. Key takeaways include:

- Plan before building, considering user roles, content types, and site purpose.
- Organize sites, libraries, and pages logically, using metadata and clear naming conventions.
- Design navigation to reflect content structure, keeping menus simple and consistent.
- Implement proper permissions, governance, and review processes to maintain long-term usability.
- Test, gather feedback, and refine the site regularly.

A well-structured site not only improves productivity but also creates a pleasant user experience, helping your team focus on work rather than hunting for information.

Chapter 4: Managing Documents and Lists

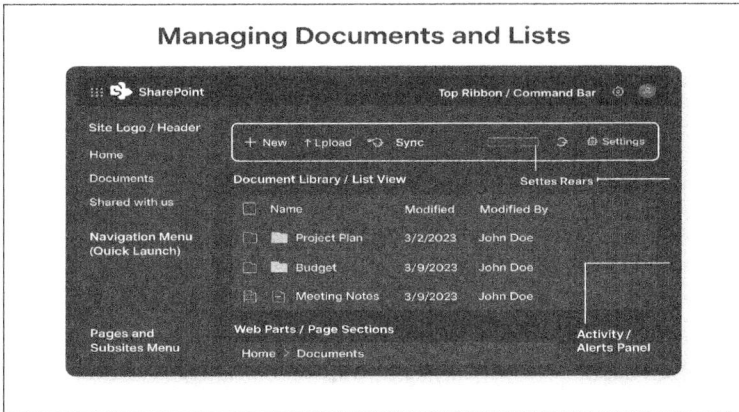

4.1 Working with Document Libraries

Document libraries are the heart of SharePoint—they are where your files live, get shared, and are managed. Think of a document library like a digital filing cabinet, but much smarter. Unlike a traditional folder on your computer, a SharePoint document library can do so much more: versioning, co-authoring, tagging, automated workflows, and advanced search capabilities. In this section, we'll go step by step, exploring all the essential features and best practices to help you confidently manage your documents and collaborate efficiently.

Understanding Document Libraries

A document library is a container for files that allows multiple users to view, edit, and collaborate in a secure environment. Every modern SharePoint site comes with at least one default library, often called **Documents**. You can create additional libraries to organize content by project, department, or function.

Key Features of Document Libraries

- **Version History:** Every change made to a document is tracked. You can restore previous versions if needed.
- **Co-Authoring:** Multiple people can edit Word, Excel, or PowerPoint files simultaneously.
- **Metadata and Tags:** Add keywords, categories, or project names to make documents easier to find.
- **Check-In/Check-Out:** Control editing by letting one person edit at a time if needed.
- **Integration with Microsoft 365:** Open and edit files directly in Office apps or Teams.

Quick Tip: Treat your libraries like a smart filing cabinet. Use folders sparingly and rely more on metadata and tags—they make searching and filtering much faster.

Step 1: Creating a Document Library

1. Go to your SharePoint site.
2. Click **Site Contents** on the left navigation menu.
3. Select **New > Document Library**.
4. Give your library a clear, descriptive name, e.g., "Marketing Assets – 2025."
5. Optionally, add a description for clarity, and choose whether to show the library in site navigation.
6. Click **Create**.

Pro Shortcut: Use consistent naming conventions for libraries, such as "Department – Function – Year," to keep everything organized and easy to locate.

Step 2: Uploading and Creating Documents

- **Upload Existing Files:** Click **Upload > Files or Folder** to add files from your computer.
- **Create New Documents:** Click **New > Word, Excel, PowerPoint, OneNote, or Link** to create a file directly in SharePoint.

Watch Out For: Avoid uploading multiple files with the same name in the same folder or library. SharePoint will add a number to the duplicate file, which can cause confusion.

Step 3: Organizing Documents

1. **Folders:** Good for broad categories (e.g., "Q1 Reports" or "Training Materials").
2. **Metadata Columns:** Add custom columns like Project Name, Document Type, Status, or Owner.
3. **Views:** Create filtered views, such as "Recent Files," "Active Projects," or "Pending Approval."

Quick Tip: Metadata is your friend! Instead of relying solely on folders, use metadata tags—it makes sorting, filtering, and searching documents much easier.

Step 4: Versioning and Document History

- **Check the Version History:** Click the ellipsis (...) next to a document and select **Version History**.
- **Restore Previous Versions:** If a mistake is made, you can roll back to an earlier version quickly.
- **Configure Version Settings:** In **Library Settings > Versioning Settings**, choose how many versions to keep for major and minor edits.

Good to Know: Version history is invaluable for collaborative projects, especially when multiple people are editing files. You never lose information, and you can track who made which changes.

Step 5: Sharing and Permissions

- **Sharing a Document:** Click **Share** next to a file. Enter email addresses or select SharePoint groups.
- **Set Permissions:** You can allow editing, read-only access, or stop sharing altogether.
- **Link Settings:** Decide if external users can view/edit the file.

Pro Shortcut: Use SharePoint groups rather than individual users to simplify permission management. For example, give your Marketing group access to all marketing-related libraries.

Step 6: Co-Authoring and Collaboration

- Open the document in **Office Online** or **desktop Office apps**.
- Multiple users can work on the same document at the same time.
- Changes are automatically saved, and you can see who is editing in real time.

Quick Tip: Encourage users to leave comments or use tracked changes when collaborating, especially on documents that require approvals or reviews.

Step 7: Automating Workflows

Document libraries integrate with **Power Automate** to automate tasks like:

- Sending notifications when a document is added or updated.
- Routing files for approval.
- Copying files to another library or team automatically.

Watch Out For: Always test your workflows before rolling them out to the entire team to ensure they behave as expected.

Step 8: Searching and Filtering

- Use the **Search Box** at the top of the library to find files quickly.
- Apply **Filters** by metadata, date modified, or file type.
- Save your filters as custom **Views** for easy access later.

Step 9: Maintaining Your Library

- Regularly archive old files to keep the library manageable.
- Review permissions to ensure only authorized users have access.
- Keep metadata and tags up to date for consistent searchability.

Good to Know: Libraries with well-organized metadata, consistent naming, and clear permissions save time and reduce user frustration.

Step 10: Best Practices for Document Libraries

- Plan your library structure in advance.
- Use descriptive names and metadata.
- Limit folder depth; rely on metadata for filtering.
- Enable versioning for all important documents.
- Set appropriate permissions from the start.
- Regularly review and clean up outdated files.

A well-managed document library transforms SharePoint from just a storage system into a collaborative powerhouse. It helps teams work efficiently, ensures data integrity, and keeps everyone on the same page. Following these steps will give your organization a solid foundation for effective document management.

4.2 Uploading, Editing, and Sharing Files

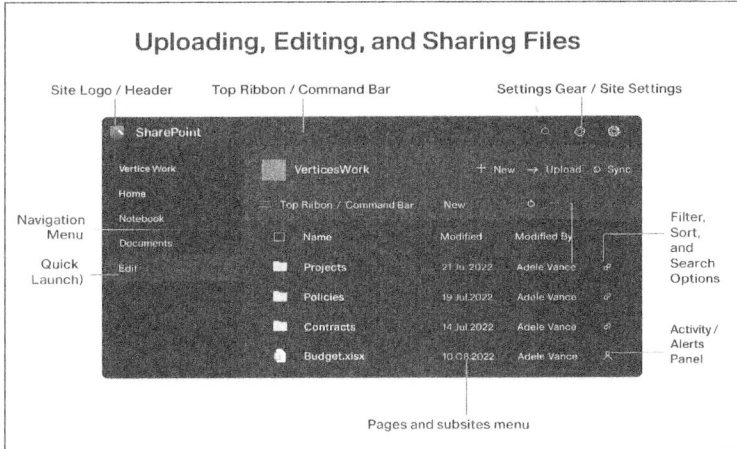

Uploading, editing, and sharing files in SharePoint is where the platform truly shines. These actions are the backbone of collaboration, allowing teams to work together seamlessly, avoid duplicate versions, and maintain a single source of truth. In this section, we'll go step by step, making sure even beginners or non-tech-savvy users feel confident navigating SharePoint's file operations.

Uploading Files

Uploading files is simple, but SharePoint offers several options depending on your workflow:

- **Drag and Drop:** Simply drag files from your computer and drop them into the document library. SharePoint will automatically upload them.
- **Upload Button:** Click **Upload > Files or Folder**. Select one or multiple files, or an entire folder.
- **Creating Files Directly in SharePoint:** Use **New > Word, Excel, PowerPoint, OneNote, or Link** to create a document inside SharePoint. This ensures the file is immediately available to all collaborators.

Watch Out For: Avoid uploading files with the same name in the same folder. SharePoint will append numbers (e.g., "Report(1).docx"), which can cause confusion.

Editing Files

Editing in SharePoint is flexible and designed to support collaboration:

- **Office Online (Browser):** Click a document to open it directly in your browser. Edits are saved automatically.
- **Desktop Apps:** Open documents in Microsoft Word, Excel, or PowerPoint. Changes sync back to SharePoint in real time.
- **Co-Authoring:** Multiple users can work on the same document simultaneously. You'll see who's editing and where, making teamwork seamless.

Quick Tip: Encourage users to leave comments or track changes in documents that require review or approval. This makes collaboration more transparent and reduces mistakes.

Sharing Files

Sharing ensures the right people have access without compromising security:

- **Sharing Within Your Organization:** Click **Share** next to a file, enter a colleague's name, and choose permissions (edit or view).
- **Sharing with External Users:** SharePoint allows you to generate links for external users. You can set expiration dates and restrict edits.
- **Link Settings:** Adjust link permissions—view-only, edit, or specific people only.

Pro Shortcut: Use SharePoint groups instead of individual email addresses when sharing. This keeps permissions organized and avoids unnecessary repetition.

Managing Permissions

- **Check Access:** See who can access a file by clicking **Manage Access**.
- **Stop Sharing:** Remove access for certain users without deleting the file.
- **Inheritance:** Permissions can be inherited from the library or customized for individual files.

Quick Tip: Regularly review file sharing and permissions to ensure sensitive information isn't overexposed.

Best Practices for Uploading, Editing, and Sharing

- Name files descriptively for easier search and retrieval.
- Use metadata and tags rather than deep folder structures.
- Keep versioning enabled to track changes and recover earlier versions.

- Communicate with your team when sharing important documents.
- Encourage co-authoring in Office Online for simultaneous editing.

By mastering these functions, your SharePoint environment becomes a powerful collaboration hub. Teams can work together efficiently, maintain a single source of truth, and protect sensitive information—all while keeping workflows smooth and intuitive.

4.3 Version History, Check-In, and Co-Authoring

One of SharePoint's most powerful features is its ability to manage documents intelligently, helping teams collaborate without confusion or accidental data loss. Version history, check-in/check-out, and co-authoring work together to ensure everyone stays on the same page—literally! Let's break these down in detail so even beginners feel confident.

Version History
Version history tracks every change made to a document, letting you see what was edited, when, and by whom. This is like having a time machine for your files.

- **Accessing Version History:** Right-click a file in a document library and select **Version History**. You'll see a list of all saved versions with timestamps and editor names.
- **Restoring Versions:** Click **Restore** on an older version to revert the document. This is incredibly useful if a mistake is made or content is accidentally deleted.
- **Good to Know:** SharePoint automatically manages version numbers, and admins can configure how many versions to retain to save storage.

Quick Tip: Encourage your team to add comments when saving major changes. This makes it easier to understand why a version was created.

Check-In and Check-Out
Check-in and check-out help prevent editing conflicts. When a user "checks

out" a document, it signals that they are making changes, preventing others from editing it simultaneously in ways that could cause conflicts.

- **Checking Out a File:** Select the file, click **Check Out**, then make edits. Other users will see the document is checked out and cannot overwrite your changes.
- **Checking In a File:** After finishing edits, click **Check In**. You can add comments to describe the changes, which then appear in version history.
- **Watch Out For:** Forgetting to check in a file can block others from editing it. SharePoint will usually warn users, but it's a good habit to check in promptly.

Pro Shortcut: Use the "Require Check Out" setting in document libraries for files that need strict editing control, such as contracts or official policies.

Co-Authoring
Co-authoring is SharePoint's solution for real-time collaboration. Multiple people can work on the same document simultaneously, with changes appearing live.

- **Office Online vs Desktop:** Co-authoring works both in Office Online (browser) and recent desktop versions of Word, Excel, and PowerPoint.
- **Seeing Collaborators:** Colored flags or initials indicate where other users are editing. This helps prevent overlaps and confusion.
- **Automatic Saves:** Changes are saved in real time, so there's no need to email files back and forth.

Quick Tip: If you experience conflicting changes, SharePoint provides a **merge feature** to reconcile differences without losing work.

Best Practices

- Encourage using **version history** for all critical documents.
- Enable **co-authoring** for teams working on reports, presentations, or collaborative projects.

- Use **check-out** for sensitive or complex documents that need controlled editing.
- Educate team members to add descriptive comments during check-in to maintain clarity.
- Regularly audit version history and permissions to avoid confusion and maintain security.

By mastering version history, check-in/check-out, and co-authoring, your SharePoint environment becomes a safe and collaborative workspace where mistakes are reversible, changes are transparent, and teamwork is seamless.

4.4 Creating and Customizing Lists

SharePoint lists are like supercharged spreadsheets—they let you organize, track, and manage information efficiently. Whether you're managing tasks, tracking inventory, or collecting feedback, lists are versatile tools that keep your team organized. Let's dive deep into how to create, customize, and optimize lists so even beginners can feel confident.

Creating a New List

1. **Navigate to Your Site:** Go to the site where you want the list.
2. **Add a New List:** Click **New > List** on the site's homepage or in the site contents menu.
3. **Choose a Template or Blank List:**
   - **Blank List:** Start fresh with no predefined columns.
   - **Templates:** Use ready-made lists like **Issue Tracker**, **Event Itinerary**, or **Contacts** for quicker setup.
4. **Name Your List:** Give your list a clear, descriptive name so team members can easily identify it. Optionally, add a description.
5. **Create Columns:** Think of columns as fields in a spreadsheet—they hold specific types of information. Examples include:
   - **Single line of text:** For names, titles, or short notes.
   - **Multiple lines of text:** For detailed descriptions or comments.

- ○ **Choice:** Drop-down menus for predefined options (e.g., Status: Pending, In Progress, Completed).
- ○ **Date and Time:** Track deadlines or event dates.
- ○ **Number:** Useful for quantities, costs, or ratings.
- ○ **Yes/No:** Simple binary choices.
6. **Save and Access Your List:** Once created, your list appears in site contents and can be accessed, edited, or shared with your team.

Customizing Your List

SharePoint allows you to tailor lists to your team's workflow for maximum efficiency.

- **Views:** Create multiple views to display your list differently. For example, a **Kanban-style board** view for tasks, a **calendar view** for deadlines, or a **filtered view** for high-priority items.
- **Sorting and Filtering:** Organize your list by specific columns like due date, status, or priority to quickly locate relevant items.
- **Conditional Formatting:** Highlight important data, such as overdue tasks or high-priority projects, using colors or icons.
- **Calculated Columns:** Perform automatic calculations like totals, averages, or due date reminders.

Quick Tip: Use **modern lists** instead of classic lists—they are more intuitive, mobile-friendly, and integrate seamlessly with Microsoft 365 tools.

Advanced List Features

- **Attachments:** Attach files to list items to provide context, such as project plans or images.
- **Integration with Power Automate:** Automate repetitive tasks like sending notifications when a list item is updated.
- **Permissions:** Control who can view, edit, or delete list items. Sensitive data can be restricted to specific team members.
- **Templates:** Once you have a list you like, save it as a template to reuse for similar projects in the future.

Tips for List Management

- Start simple and add complexity gradually—don't overwhelm yourself or your team with too many columns at once.
- Name columns clearly and consistently to avoid confusion.
- Encourage your team to keep list items updated regularly.
- Use **views and filters** to focus on what matters most.
- Periodically review lists to archive completed or outdated items to keep things organized.

By mastering SharePoint lists, your team gains a powerful tool to track projects, manage workflows, and keep information accessible in a structured way. With customization, automation, and thoughtful design, lists become more than just data—they become an engine for productivity and collaboration.

4.5 Views, Filters, and Metadata

One of SharePoint's most powerful features is the ability to organize and display information exactly how you need it. Views, filters, and metadata help you transform a standard list or library into a dynamic, easy-to-navigate workspace. Let's explore these features in detail so you can confidently manage your content.

Views: Displaying Information Your Way

Views let you see the same list or library in multiple ways without creating duplicate data. Think of views as different "lenses" that show the information that matters most for a particular task or audience.

- **Creating a New View:**

  1. Go to the list or library.
  2. Click **All Items** (or the current view name) and select **Create new view**.
  3. Choose a format:
     - **Standard View:** Lists items vertically, similar to a spreadsheet.

- **Calendar View:** Displays items with dates on a calendar—perfect for deadlines and events.
- **Gallery View:** Shows items visually, ideal for images or portfolios.
- **Board View (Kanban):** Organizes items by status or category in columns for task management.
4. Name your view and set visibility (personal or public).
- **Quick Tip:** Use **personal views** for your own workflow and **public views** when you want the whole team to see the same arrangement.

Filters: Focus on What Matters

Filters let you temporarily narrow down items in a list or library. For example, you might only want to see tasks that are overdue, or documents authored by a specific person.

- **Applying a Filter:**
  1. Open your list or library.
  2. Click the column header you want to filter by.
  3. Select the criteria (e.g., "Status = In Progress" or "Department = Marketing").
- **Advanced Filters:** Combine multiple conditions to create highly specific views.

Metadata: Adding Context and Organization

Metadata is information about your items—like tags on social media. Unlike filenames, metadata can include multiple details, such as category, project, department, or priority. Metadata helps you search, filter, and sort items more effectively.

- **Adding Metadata:**

  ○ When creating a new column, think of it as metadata. For example, a **Project Name** column or a **Document Type** column.

- ○ Tag existing items using **Quick Edit** mode or via item properties.
- **Benefits of Metadata:**

  - ○ Makes searching faster and more accurate.
  - ○ Enables dynamic views and filtering.
  - ○ Reduces reliance on long, complex filenames.

Combining Views, Filters, and Metadata

- You can create a **view that shows only high-priority tasks** by combining metadata and filters.
- Metadata allows you to **group items** in views (e.g., group documents by department).
- Filters let you temporarily tweak the view to focus on a subset of data without changing the underlying structure.

Good to Know: Views can also include **sorting**, **conditional formatting**, and even **color coding**, giving you a clear visual representation of your data.

Pro Shortcut: Use the modern SharePoint interface's **column settings and quick filters** to adjust views without entering advanced settings.

By mastering views, filters, and metadata, you can turn a simple SharePoint list or library into a tailored, easy-to-navigate workspace. Your team will be able to find what they need faster, stay organized, and work more efficiently.

Chapter 5: Collaboration and Communication

5.1 Sharing and Permissions Management

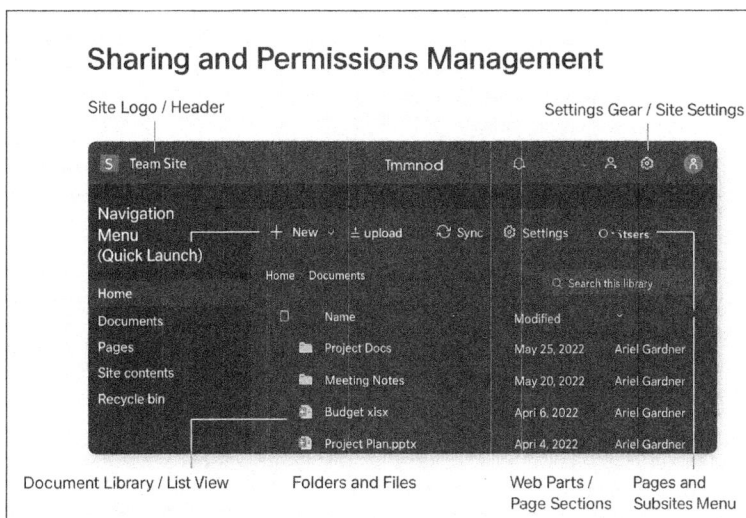

Sharing and Permissions Management

Site Logo / Header — Settings Gear / Site Settings

Navigation Menu (Quick Launch)

Document Library / List View — Folders and Files — Web Parts / Page Sections — Pages and Subsites Menu

One of SharePoint's most valuable strengths is enabling seamless collaboration. Whether you're working with a small team or an entire organization, SharePoint lets you share documents, sites, and information securely while controlling who can see, edit, or manage your content. In this section, we'll explore **sharing options, permissions levels, best practices, and real-world tips** to make collaboration both easy and safe.

Understanding Sharing in SharePoint

Sharing is how you give others access to content stored in SharePoint. It's not just about sending a link; it's about controlling **who can do what** with your documents, libraries, or entire sites.

- **Types of Sharing:**

  - **Internal Sharing:** Share content with people inside your organization.
  - **External Sharing:** Invite guests or partners outside your organization. SharePoint makes it possible to grant temporary or limited access without compromising security.
  - **Link-Based Sharing:** Share via a link that can have **view-only**, **edit**, or **co-owner** permissions.
- **Quick Tip:** For sensitive documents, avoid using "Anyone with the link" sharing. Instead, invite specific people to maintain control.

Permissions Levels Explained

SharePoint uses **role-based permissions** to manage access. Here's a breakdown of the main levels:

- **Read:** Can view content but cannot make changes.
- **Contribute:** Can view, add, and edit items, but cannot delete or manage permissions.
- **Edit:** Can view, add, edit, and delete items in a library or list.
- **Full Control / Owner:** Has complete control over the site, including managing permissions, site settings, and content.

Pro Shortcut: Use **SharePoint Groups** instead of assigning permissions individually. Groups like **Members**, **Owners**, and **Visitors** simplify management and reduce errors.

Sharing Files and Folders Step-by-Step

1. **Locate the File or Folder:** Navigate to your library and select the item you want to share.
2. **Click Share:** The sharing pane will appear with link options.
3. **Choose Link Type:**
   - **People in your organization:** Internal team members only.
   - **Specific people:** Only the people you specify can access.

- ○ **Anyone with the link:** External sharing (check your organization's policy).
4. **Set Permissions:** Decide if recipients can **edit** or **view only**.
5. **Add a Message (Optional):** Give context or instructions to recipients.
6. **Send or Copy Link:** Send directly from SharePoint or copy the link to paste into email or chat.

Managing Site Permissions

Sharing a single file is easy, but site-level permissions ensure your **entire team or project** has the correct access:

- **Step 1:** Navigate to **Site Settings > Site Permissions**.
- **Step 2:** Review existing **Groups and Members**.
- **Step 3:** Add new members to the appropriate group (Owners, Members, Visitors).
- **Step 4:** Remove or adjust access for former team members or external users.

Good to Know: Permissions in SharePoint are **cumulative**. If a user belongs to multiple groups, they get the **highest level of access** granted. Always review carefully to avoid unintended access.

Tips for Safe and Effective Collaboration

- **Organize by Teams and Projects:** Create separate libraries for different teams or projects to avoid clutter and accidental sharing.
- **Set Expiration Dates for External Links:** Reduce risk by limiting access duration.
- **Monitor Access:** Regularly check who has access to sensitive documents. Use the **Access Requests** feature to review pending invitations.
- **Use Alerts:** Set up notifications to stay informed when documents are changed or shared.
- **Version Control:** Enable versioning so changes can be tracked and reverted if needed.

Real-World Example:

Imagine a marketing team working on a campaign. They create a SharePoint library with folders for **Graphics**, **Content**, and **Reports**. Each folder has tailored permissions:

- **Graphics folder:** Designers can edit, Marketing team can view.
- **Content folder:** All team members can edit.
- **Reports folder:** Only managers have edit rights, everyone else has read-only access.

This setup ensures that team members collaborate efficiently without overwriting each other's work or accessing files they shouldn't.

Watch Out For:

- Avoid sharing **sensitive HR or finance documents** using generic links. Always use specific people links and strong permissions.
- Don't forget to **review external guest access** periodically. Access that isn't managed can linger and create security risks.

By mastering **sharing and permissions**, you empower your team to collaborate seamlessly while keeping your organization's data safe and well-organized. Properly managed, SharePoint becomes a powerful hub for teamwork and productivity.

5.2 Using News Posts and Announcements

SharePoint isn't just for storing files—it's also a **dynamic communication platform** that helps your team stay informed and engaged. With **news posts** and **announcements**, you can share updates, celebrate milestones, or broadcast important information across your organization. In this section, we'll dive into how to **create, manage, and optimize news posts and announcements**, ensuring your messages reach the right people in the most effective way.

Understanding News Posts vs. Announcements

- **News Posts:** Designed for **dynamic content** like project updates, team achievements, or important organizational news. News posts are visually rich, can include images, videos, links, and are automatically highlighted on your site's homepage.
- **Announcements:** Ideal for **short, quick messages**, such as reminders, alerts, or upcoming events. Announcements are simpler than news posts and can be pinned to specific pages or displayed in web parts.

Quick Tip: Think of news posts as your team's newsletter and announcements as your internal bulletin board. Both help keep everyone aligned, but they serve slightly different purposes.

Creating a News Post Step-by-Step

1. **Navigate to Your SharePoint Site:** Go to the site where you want to publish your news post.
2. **Select "New" > "News Post":** This opens a page where you can start creating your content.
3. **Add a Catchy Title:** Make it clear and engaging—this is what readers will see first.
4. **Insert Content:** Use **text, images, videos, links, or embedded documents** to make your post visually appealing.
   - **Pro Shortcut:** Use **web parts** like Hero, Quick Links, or Image Gallery to structure content beautifully.
5. **Set the Layout:** Choose from layout options like **One column, Two columns, or Top story** to organize your information.
6. **Publish:** Click **Publish** to make your post live immediately, or **Schedule** it for a future date.

Using Announcements Effectively

- Announcements are typically added via the **Announcements list** or a dedicated web part on a site page.
- **Steps to Add an Announcement:**

1. Navigate to the **Announcements list**.
2. Click **New** to create an announcement.
3. Enter a **Title**, **Body**, and optionally **Add a link or image**.
4. Set a **Start and End date** if it's time-sensitive.
5. Save or publish the announcement.

Good to Know: Announcements can automatically display in a **rolling feed** on your homepage, keeping your site looking fresh and ensuring critical messages aren't missed.

Optimizing for Engagement

- **Use Visuals:** Images or videos make your news posts more engaging. A picture really is worth a thousand words!
- **Highlight Key Points:** Use **bold text or headings** to draw attention to important information.
- **Keep it Concise:** While news posts can be longer, announcements should be **short and to the point**.
- **Leverage Targeting:** SharePoint allows you to target news posts to specific **groups or departments**, ensuring relevant content reaches the right audience.
- **Encourage Interaction:** Enable **comments or reactions** to foster engagement and feedback.

Real-World Example:

Imagine a company launching a new product. A **news post** can highlight the product's features with images and a launch video. Meanwhile, an **announcement** can remind all employees about the launch webinar or training session. Together, they ensure that everyone is informed, engaged, and ready for the launch.

Watch Out For:

- Avoid posting duplicate announcements across multiple pages—it can confuse readers.
- Regularly **archive old posts and announcements** to keep your site clean and focused.

- Make sure you **proofread and fact-check** content before publishing; once it's live, it's visible to your whole team.

By mastering **news posts and announcements**, you can make your SharePoint site a **central hub for communication**, keep your team aligned, and foster a culture of transparency and engagement.

5.3 Discussion Boards, Calendars, and Alerts

SharePoint isn't just a file repository—it's a **collaboration powerhouse**. Features like **discussion boards, calendars, and alerts** help teams stay connected, organized, and proactive. Let's explore how each tool works and how you can use them effectively to streamline communication and project management.

Discussion Boards: Fostering Team Conversations

Discussion boards are like **virtual meeting spaces** where team members can ask questions, share ideas, or brainstorm without sending endless email chains. They help maintain a **centralized conversation history** that everyone can reference.

Creating and Using Discussion Boards

1. **Navigate to Your Site:** Go to the site where you want to create the discussion board.
2. **Add a Discussion Board App:** Click **New > App > Discussion Board**. Give it a **clear name** like "Marketing Ideas" or "Project Q&A."
3. **Start a New Discussion:** Click **New Discussion** and enter a **title and message**. Encourage team members to reply rather than start new threads unless the topic is different.
4. **Organize by Categories:** Categories or tags help keep conversations **structured and easy to find**.

Quick Tip: Treat discussion boards like a **forum for your team**. Encourage respectful and constructive interactions and regularly check for unanswered posts.

Calendars: Keeping Everyone on Track

SharePoint calendars allow you to **schedule events, deadlines, and team meetings** in one central location. Unlike individual calendars, these are **team-wide** and accessible from any device.

Setting Up a SharePoint Calendar

1. **Navigate to the Site:** Open the site where the calendar should live.
2. **Add a Calendar App:** Click **New > App > Calendar**, and give it a descriptive name.
3. **Add Events:** Click **New Event**, enter the **title, date, time, and location**, and optionally add **reminders or categories**.
4. **Overlay with Outlook:** You can **connect your SharePoint calendar to Outlook**, so team members can view and manage events from one place.

Pro Shortcut: Use **color-coded categories** for different types of events (meetings, deadlines, milestones) for instant visual recognition.

Alerts: Staying Informed Automatically

Alerts help team members **stay on top of updates** without constantly checking SharePoint. You can set alerts for **documents, lists, libraries, or entire sites**.

Setting Up Alerts

1. Navigate to the **document library, list, or discussion board** you want alerts for.
2. Click **... (More Options) > Alert Me > Set Alert on this Library/List**.
3. Choose your **alert settings**, including:
   ○ **Delivery method:** Email or SMS (if configured)
   ○ **Change type:** All changes, new items, or modifications
   ○ **Frequency:** Immediate, daily summary, or weekly summary
4. Click **OK** to activate the alert.

Good to Know: Alerts are a gentle way to **automate notifications** so no one misses critical updates, approvals, or new conversations.

Real-World Example:
Imagine a project team coordinating a product launch:

- The **discussion board** is used to brainstorm marketing ideas and ask questions.
- The **team calendar** schedules deadlines, review meetings, and launch events.
- **Alerts** notify team members whenever a key document is updated or a new discussion thread is added.

Watch Out For:

- Avoid overwhelming your team with too many alerts; focus on **critical updates only**.
- Regularly **review old calendar events and discussion threads** to keep the site organized.
- Ensure everyone knows how to **reply to discussions** correctly to maintain coherent threads.

By mastering **discussion boards, calendars, and alerts**, you can transform SharePoint into a **centralized hub for communication, scheduling, and real-time updates**, reducing emails and boosting productivity.

5.4 Integrating SharePoint with Teams and Outlook

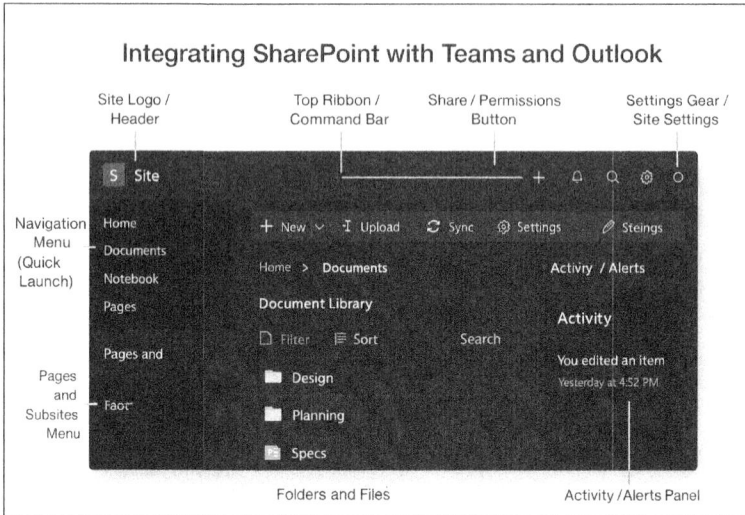

Integrating SharePoint with Teams and Outlook

SharePoint is powerful on its own, but its true potential shines when integrated with **Microsoft Teams and Outlook**. These integrations create a **seamless workspace**, where your files, conversations, and calendars live in one place—making teamwork simpler, faster, and less fragmented. Let's break down how to get the most out of these integrations.

Why Integration Matters

Think of SharePoint as the **central library** of your organization. Teams acts as the **meeting room and chat space**, and Outlook is your **personal assistant for emails and scheduling**. When all three work together, you get:

- **Single access to documents** without switching apps
- **Real-time collaboration** on files and projects
- **Automatic notifications** for updates, meetings, and tasks
- **Consistent communication** across channels

Integrating SharePoint with Teams

1. **Add a SharePoint Site to Teams:**

   - Open **Microsoft Teams**.
   - Navigate to the **team** where you want to link SharePoint.
   - Click **+ (Add a Tab)** at the top of the channel.
   - Choose **Document Library** or **SharePoint**.
   - Select the **site or library** you want to link.
   - Now, your SharePoint documents appear **directly inside Teams**, ready for collaboration.

2. **Collaborate in Real-Time:**

   - Teams allows you to **open, edit, and co-author SharePoint documents** without leaving the app.
   - Comments, chat, and version history are preserved, giving **context to every change**.

3. **Pin Important Libraries or Lists:**

   - Pin frequently used SharePoint libraries as **tabs in Teams** for easy access.
   - Use **Teams notifications** to alert members about changes or updates.

Quick Tip: Treat the Teams channel as a **hub for your SharePoint content**, so your team always knows where to find important files.

Integrating SharePoint with Outlook

1. **Access SharePoint Calendars in Outlook:**

   - Navigate to the **SharePoint calendar** you want to sync.
   - Click **Calendar > Connect to Outlook**.
   - Outlook will display your SharePoint calendar alongside your personal calendar, allowing you to **see deadlines, meetings, and events in one view**.

2. **Subscribe to SharePoint Alerts in Outlook:**

   - Alerts set in SharePoint can **deliver emails directly to your Outlook inbox**, keeping you informed of changes, new documents, or discussion updates.

3. **Drag-and-Drop Emails to SharePoint:**

   - Outlook allows you to **save important emails or attachments** directly to SharePoint libraries.
   - Simply **drag the email** into a synced SharePoint folder or use the **"Move to" option**.
   - This keeps project-related communication **together with files and documentation**.

Pro Shortcut: Use **Outlook rules** to automatically organize incoming SharePoint notifications into dedicated folders—reducing inbox clutter and keeping updates easy to find.

Real-World Example:
Imagine you are working on a marketing campaign:

- **Teams channel**: Team chats, brainstorming, and file collaboration happen here.
- **SharePoint library**: All campaign assets (images, documents, and templates) are stored here.
- **Outlook**: Alerts notify you of new file uploads, upcoming deadlines, and meeting invitations.

With this setup, everyone is **on the same page**, and files never get lost in email threads.

Watch Out For:

- Ensure **permissions are correctly set** in SharePoint before linking to Teams, or members may not access files.
- Avoid linking **too many libraries** at once in Teams to prevent clutter.

- Remember that syncing SharePoint calendars to Outlook may **require occasional refreshes** if there are changes to the library structure.

By integrating SharePoint with Teams and Outlook, you create a **connected digital workspace** where collaboration is smoother, communication is centralized, and projects stay on track.

Chapter 6: Automating and Integrating

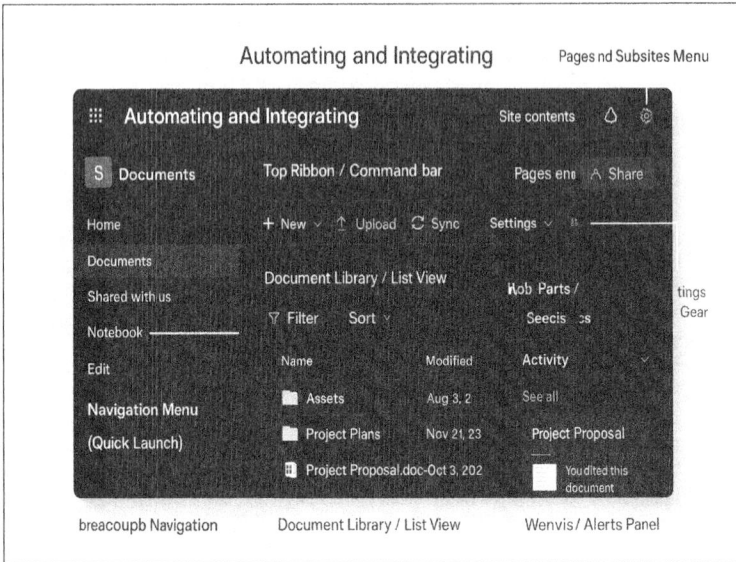

6.1 Using Power Automate for Workflows

Power Automate is SharePoint's **built-in automation engine**, designed to help you **save time, reduce repetitive tasks, and streamline business processes**. Think of it as your digital assistant that can **move files, send notifications, and update systems automatically**, freeing you to focus on higher-value work.

Why Power Automate Matters
Imagine having a helper who can:

- Send emails whenever a document is updated
- Move files to the right folders based on content type

- Notify a team when a task is completed
  That's exactly what Power Automate does—and it works **seamlessly with SharePoint, Teams, Outlook, and hundreds of other apps**.

Getting Started: The Basics

- **Step 1: Access Power Automate**

  - From SharePoint, click the **Automate** menu on a document library.
  - Select **Power Automate → Create a flow**.
  - You can also go directly to flow.microsoft.com to explore templates.

- **Step 2: Choose a Template or Start from Scratch**

  - **Templates:** Pre-built workflows like "Send a notification when a file is added" or "Copy files from one library to another."
  - **From scratch:** Build a custom flow tailored to your exact process.

- **Step 3: Define the Trigger**

  - Triggers are events that start the workflow. Examples:
    - A new file is uploaded
    - A list item is modified
    - A form is submitted
  - Quick Tip: Think of triggers as the **starting signal for your automation**.

- **Step 4: Add Actions**

  - Actions are tasks the workflow performs after it's triggered. Examples:
    - Send an email or Teams message
    - Create or update list items
    - Move or copy files

○ You can add multiple actions in sequence or parallel for complex workflows.

Example Workflow: Document Approval Process

1. **Trigger:** A new file is uploaded to a document library.
2. **Action 1:** Notify the manager via email.
3. **Action 2:** Wait for approval response.
4. **Action 3a:** If approved, move the file to the "Approved" folder and notify the team.
5. **Action 3b:** If rejected, move the file to the "Needs Review" folder and notify the submitter.
   This automation **reduces delays, ensures accountability, and eliminates manual tracking**.

Customizing Workflows for Your Team

- Use **conditions** to create "if-then" logic. Example: If the document type is "Invoice," notify the finance team; otherwise, notify the project manager.
- Include **loops** for repetitive actions, such as sending notifications for multiple files.
- Utilize **dynamic content** from SharePoint or other connected apps to personalize messages and actions automatically.

Monitoring and Managing Flows

- Once your flow is active, go to Power Automate → **My Flows** to check **run history**, **errors**, and performance.
- Quick Tip: Name flows clearly with the purpose and date to keep them organized.
- Watch Out For: Large or complex flows can slow down execution—optimize steps and avoid unnecessary actions.

Good to Know:

- Power Automate integrates with **over 400 apps**, including Teams, Outlook, OneDrive, Excel, and even third-party services like Slack, Salesforce, and Twitter.
- **Templates save time** for beginners, but as you gain confidence, building flows from scratch provides maximum flexibility.
- **Error handling:** Add "configure run after" steps to manage failed actions gracefully. For instance, if sending an email fails, log it in a SharePoint list for later review.

Tips for Beginners:

- Start small: automate simple tasks like email notifications or file moves.
- Test flows thoroughly with sample files before going live.
- Encourage your team to provide feedback—sometimes automation uncovers gaps in your processes you hadn't noticed.

Pro Shortcut: Use the **"Copy a Flow" feature** to replicate workflows across different sites or libraries—this is great when you have multiple teams following similar processes.

Real-World Applications:

- HR onboarding: Automatically send welcome emails, assign tasks, and notify IT to set up accounts.
- Project management: Track task completion, update status dashboards, and notify stakeholders.
- Document control: Automate approvals, archive outdated files, and alert teams to updates.

Power Automate **turns repetitive work into a set-it-and-forget-it system**, letting your team focus on creativity, decision-making, and collaboration. With practice, even beginners can design sophisticated workflows that **save hours each week and make SharePoint a truly collaborative, efficient environment**.

6.2 Connecting SharePoint with Power Apps

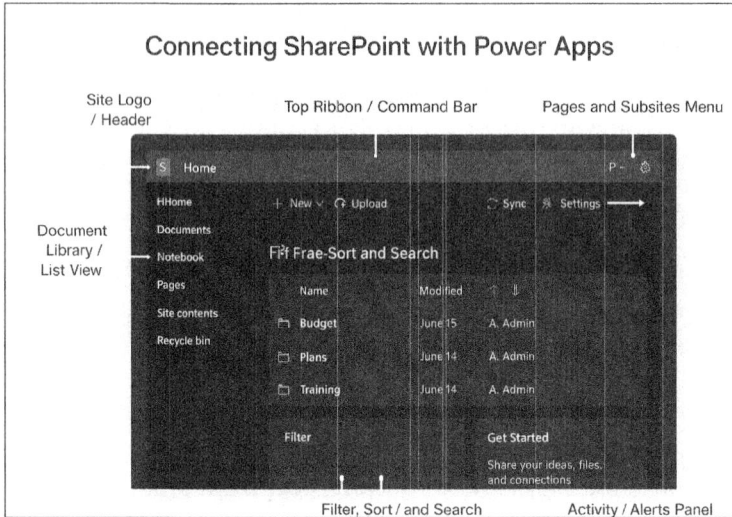

Connecting SharePoint with Power Apps

Power Apps is Microsoft's **low-code platform** that allows you to build **custom apps** tailored to your organization's needs. When combined with SharePoint, it **turns your lists and libraries into interactive apps** that team members can use on any device—desktop, tablet, or mobile. Think of it as **transforming your SharePoint data into a user-friendly app without writing tons of code**.

Why Connect SharePoint to Power Apps

- SharePoint lists and libraries often hold critical information, but navigating them in the default interface can be slow or cumbersome.
- Power Apps creates a **streamlined, visually intuitive interface**, making data entry, updates, and reporting faster and easier.
- It enables **mobile access**, so your team can work on the go without being tied to a computer.

- You can add **logic, rules, and automated workflows** inside the app to reduce errors and ensure consistency.

Getting Started: Step-by-Step

Step 1: Identify the SharePoint Data Source

- Decide which **list or library** you want your app to connect to.
- Quick Tip: Start with a smaller list to make testing easier before scaling to larger data sets.

Step 2: Launch Power Apps

- From your SharePoint list, click Integrate → Power Apps → Create an App.
- Give your app a meaningful name, like "Project Tracker" or "HR Onboarding App."
- Power Apps will automatically generate a **default three-screen app**: browse, details, and edit screens.

Step 3: Explore the Generated App

- **Browse screen:** Lets users see all items in your SharePoint list.
- **Detail screen:** Shows all information about a selected item.
- **Edit screen:** Allows adding or updating items directly.
- Watch Out For: The auto-generated layout may need adjustments for usability, especially if your list has many columns.

Step 4: Customize Your App

- Use drag-and-drop controls like **buttons, text boxes, dropdowns, and galleries** to rearrange the layout.
- Quick Tip: Rename fields clearly so users understand what each column represents.
- Add **conditional formatting** to highlight important items, e.g., overdue tasks in red.
- Insert **media**, like images or icons, to make the app visually engaging.

Step 5: Add Logic and Automation

- You can incorporate simple formulas similar to Excel, e.g.,
  `If(Status="Completed", "Green", "Red")`.
- Connect your app to **Power Automate flows** to trigger actions automatically, like sending notifications or creating tasks when data changes.
- Pro Shortcut: Use **rules and validation** to prevent incorrect data entry, reducing errors.

Step 6: Test Your App

- Preview the app inside Power Apps Studio using the **Play button**.
- Test all screens, inputs, and workflows to ensure they behave as expected.
- Good to Know: Testing on mobile devices is crucial, as layout or navigation may differ from the desktop view.

Step 7: Share and Publish

- Once satisfied, click File → Save → Publish.
- Share with your team or organization by assigning **permissions** in Power Apps.
- Watch Out For: Users need proper SharePoint and Power Apps licenses to access the app.

Real-World Use Cases

- **Project Management:** Track tasks, deadlines, and status updates directly from a SharePoint list, all in a mobile-friendly app.
- **HR Onboarding:** Create an app where HR can input new employee details, assign equipment, and automatically trigger welcome emails.
- **Inventory Management:** Employees can update stock levels, log new shipments, and view reports—all from a customized app linked to SharePoint libraries.

Tips for Beginners

- Start simple: Use one list and three screens. Add complexity gradually.
- Use **clear, descriptive labels** and avoid cluttered screens to make it intuitive.
- Preview frequently: Always test your app as you make changes to catch issues early.
- Document your app structure: Helps you maintain it and onboard new team members.

Quick Tip: Use **Power Apps templates** if you want a head start. Many common business scenarios are already pre-built and can be customized to your organization's needs.

By connecting SharePoint with Power Apps, you **empower your team to interact with data in a way that's more efficient, engaging, and mobile-friendly**, turning your lists and libraries into dynamic, action-oriented tools.

6.3 Automating Approvals and Notifications

One of SharePoint's most powerful capabilities is **automation**. By setting up approvals and notifications, your team can **move faster, reduce manual errors, and ensure that critical tasks never get overlooked**. Whether it's a leave request, document review, or project update, automation helps your workflows run smoothly without constant oversight.

Why Automate Approvals and Notifications

- **Save time:** Manual follow-ups are eliminated. The system automatically alerts the right people.
- **Increase accountability:** Every step is tracked and documented, so you know who approved or rejected an item.
- **Reduce errors:** Automated workflows ensure processes are followed correctly.
- **Improve visibility:** Everyone involved knows the status of approvals in real time.

Getting Started: Using Power Automate

Power Automate (formerly Microsoft Flow) is SharePoint's automation companion. It allows you to **create automated workflows** that connect SharePoint with email, Teams, and other apps.

Step 1: Identify the Workflow

- Decide what you want to automate. Examples: document approvals, leave requests, purchase orders, or status updates.
- Quick Tip: Start with one simple workflow to get familiar with the interface.

Step 2: Open Power Automate

- From your SharePoint list or library, click **Automate** → **Power Automate** → **Create a Flow**.
- Choose **"Start from blank"** or select a template like **"Request approval for a new item"**.

Step 3: Set Up Triggers

- A trigger is an event that starts the workflow, such as **when a new item is created or modified** in SharePoint.
- Watch Out For: Ensure your trigger corresponds exactly to the action you want automated. Otherwise, the workflow may run too often or miss updates.

Step 4: Add Approval Steps

- Use the **"Start and wait for an approval"** action.
- Choose the approval type:
  - **Approve/Reject – First to respond**: Workflow moves forward when any approver responds.
  - **Approve/Reject – Everyone must approve**: Workflow waits until all approvers respond.
- Assign **approvers** by email or use a dynamic field from your SharePoint list.

- Good to Know: You can customize the approval message to include context, attachments, or instructions.

Step 5: Configure Notifications

- After each step, add **notification actions** to alert team members. Common options include:
  - **Send an email**: Automatically notify when an item is approved, rejected, or pending.
  - **Post a message in Microsoft Teams**: Keeps teams informed without leaving their chat platform.
  - **Send push notifications to mobile devices** for urgent approvals.
- Pro Shortcut: Use dynamic content from SharePoint, such as item name or requester, to make notifications personalized.

Step 6: Add Conditional Logic

- Conditional actions allow workflows to behave differently based on certain criteria.
- Example: If a document is marked "High Priority," send notifications to managers immediately; otherwise, follow the standard approval chain.
- Quick Tip: Use **"Conditions"** in Power Automate to create rules without coding.

Step 7: Test and Refine Your Workflow

- Click **Test** to simulate item creation and track how approvals and notifications behave.
- Adjust the workflow if emails are sent incorrectly or if approval steps are skipped.
- Watch Out For: Remember that workflows only apply to new or modified items, so test with multiple scenarios.

Step 8: Monitor Workflow Performance

- Power Automate provides **run history logs** where you can see every action taken, who approved, and when notifications were sent.
- Good to Know: Monitoring helps identify bottlenecks or missed approvals and ensures accountability.

Real-World Examples

- **Document Approval:** A marketing team uploads content to SharePoint; the manager receives an automated approval request. Once approved, the content is published, and notifications are sent to the team.
- **Leave Request:** Employees submit leave requests through SharePoint; HR and the manager are notified, approvals are tracked, and the calendar is automatically updated.
- **Purchase Orders:** Requests for supplies are routed through the finance team; each step triggers notifications until the order is completed.

Tips for Beginners

- Start simple: Begin with a single approval step before adding multiple conditions or nested logic.
- Use templates: Power Automate has many prebuilt approval flows suitable for common business processes.
- Keep users informed: Always include clear instructions in notifications so approvers know exactly what to do.
- Document your workflows: Helps team members understand and maintain them over time.

Quick Tip: Combining **SharePoint with Power Automate and Teams** creates a **seamless workflow experience**. Teams get instant notifications, SharePoint keeps records, and Power Automate ensures nothing falls through the cracks.

6.4 Integrating with OneDrive, Planner, and Viva Connections

SharePoint becomes even more powerful when you connect it with other Microsoft 365 apps like **OneDrive, Planner, and Viva Connections**. These integrations allow teams to **collaborate seamlessly, manage tasks efficiently, and keep everyone informed** without leaving the SharePoint environment. Whether you're a beginner or someone who hasn't explored Microsoft 365 fully, these integrations can streamline your workflow significantly.

Why Integrate?

- **Centralized Work:** All your files, tasks, and updates can be accessed from SharePoint, reducing the need to switch apps constantly.
- **Improved Collaboration:** Teams can co-author documents in real-time via OneDrive, track tasks in Planner, and stay updated with company news through Viva Connections.
- **Efficiency & Accountability:** Integration ensures everyone knows what they need to do, when, and with which documents or resources.

Step 1: OneDrive Integration

OneDrive is your personal cloud storage within Microsoft 365. When integrated with SharePoint:

- You can **sync document libraries** so files stored in SharePoint are accessible offline from your device.
- **Co-author documents in real-time**, even if teammates are editing simultaneously.
- **Quick Access:** Files you frequently use in SharePoint can appear in OneDrive, giving you a familiar and organized interface.

How to Set It Up:

1. Open a SharePoint document library.
2. Click **Sync** at the top of the library. This will prompt OneDrive to synchronize the folder.

3. Files will appear in your OneDrive folder on your computer, automatically updating when changes are made online.

Quick Tip: Use OneDrive's **"Files On-Demand"** feature to save storage space. You can see all files in File Explorer without downloading them until needed.

Step 2: Planner Integration

Planner helps teams **organize tasks visually** using boards, buckets, and cards. Integrating Planner with SharePoint allows you to:

- Assign tasks linked to SharePoint projects or documents.
- Track task progress directly from SharePoint pages using Planner web parts.
- Automate notifications so team members are alerted when deadlines approach or tasks are updated.

How to Add Planner to SharePoint:

1. Navigate to the SharePoint page where you want to display tasks.
2. Click **Edit Page** → **Add a Web Part** → **Planner**.
3. Choose an existing plan or create a new one.
4. Customize columns, buckets, and task assignments directly from SharePoint.

Pro Shortcut: Combine Planner with **Power Automate** to trigger workflows. For example, when a task is marked "Completed," SharePoint can automatically update related documents or notify stakeholders.

Step 3: Viva Connections Integration

Viva Connections is Microsoft's **employee experience platform** that brings company news, resources, and dashboards directly into Microsoft Teams and SharePoint. Integrating Viva Connections with SharePoint helps:

- Share organizational announcements and news on your SharePoint intranet.

- Highlight key resources, policies, and dashboards in a single, easy-to-access hub.
- Encourage engagement by providing quick links and interactive content without leaving SharePoint.

How to Add Viva Connections:

1. Ensure you have **Viva Connections Dashboard** set up in Microsoft 365 admin center.
2. Add **Viva Connections web parts** to your SharePoint site.
3. Customize cards, links, and news posts to match your company's needs.

Good to Know: Viva Connections can be personalized for each employee, showing content relevant to their role or department. This ensures the SharePoint site isn't just a repository but a dynamic, engaging portal.

Tips for Beginners:

- Start small: Sync one library in OneDrive, add a Planner board for a single project, and experiment with a simple Viva Connections card.
- Use templates: Microsoft 365 offers prebuilt templates for Planner and Viva Connections to make setup easier.
- Educate your team: Provide a quick guide or short video so everyone understands how to access integrated tools.
- Monitor usage: Check which integrations are most helpful and adjust as needed to reduce clutter.

Watch Out For: Ensure users have proper permissions for each integration. For instance, someone might have access to SharePoint but not Planner or OneDrive, which can create confusion.

Step 4: Maximizing Efficiency with Combined Use

- Upload files in SharePoint → Sync via OneDrive for offline access.
- Create tasks in Planner linked to those files → Assign team members.

- Share updates and news through Viva Connections → Keep everyone informed of project milestones.

Quick Tip: Think of SharePoint as your **hub**, OneDrive as your **personal workspace**, Planner as your **task manager**, and Viva Connections as your **company bulletin board**. Together, they create a **seamless, efficient, and collaborative environment**.

6.5 Leveraging Microsoft 365 Tools Together

SharePoint shines when used as part of the **broader Microsoft 365 ecosystem**, allowing teams to work smarter, not harder. Leveraging tools like **Teams, OneDrive, Outlook, Planner, Power Automate, Power Apps, and Viva Connections together with SharePoint** creates a seamless workflow where files, tasks, communications, and data are all interconnected. This chapter will walk you through how to combine these tools effectively, making SharePoint a **central hub** for productivity while keeping everyone on the same page.

Why Integrate Microsoft 365 Tools?

- **Centralized Collaboration:** Your documents, meetings, emails, and tasks all live in one interconnected environment.
- **Time-Saving Automation:** Automate repetitive processes, such as approvals, notifications, and data collection.
- **Improved Communication:** Real-time updates and alerts keep everyone informed and reduce the need for long email chains.
- **Better Decision Making:** Data collected across tools can be analyzed and presented directly in SharePoint using **Power BI** dashboards.

Step 1: SharePoint + Teams

Teams and SharePoint work hand-in-hand. Every Teams channel automatically creates a corresponding SharePoint document library. Benefits include:

- **File Management:** Files shared in Teams are stored in SharePoint, providing version history and co-authoring capabilities.
- **Quick Access:** Teams users can access SharePoint libraries directly without leaving the Teams interface.
- **Team Pages:** Use SharePoint to build intranet pages for departments or projects, and link them in Teams tabs for easy navigation.

How to Connect:

1. Open your Teams channel → Click **Files** → **Open in SharePoint.**
2. Customize your SharePoint site to reflect project resources or team documentation.
3. Pin the SharePoint site as a tab in Teams for instant access.

Quick Tip: Think of Teams as your **chat room and meeting space**, while SharePoint is the **library and project hub**. Linking them reduces duplicated work and keeps files in a single source of truth.

Step 2: SharePoint + OneDrive

OneDrive is your **personal storage**, while SharePoint serves as your **team or organization repository**. Integrating them ensures:

- **Offline Access:** Sync SharePoint libraries to OneDrive to access and edit documents even without an internet connection.
- **Seamless Collaboration:** Co-author documents in real-time, with changes automatically updated across OneDrive and SharePoint.

Pro Shortcut: Use OneDrive's **"Shared Libraries"** to quickly navigate between personal and team files without searching manually.

Step 3: SharePoint + Planner

Planner integration allows you to turn project tasks into **visual boards** linked to SharePoint sites. This is perfect for:

- Managing project timelines and deadlines.
- Assigning tasks to team members with automatic notifications.

- Displaying Planner boards directly on SharePoint pages via web parts.

Step 4: SharePoint + Power Automate

Power Automate enables you to create **workflows that save time and reduce errors**, such as:

- Automating document approvals in SharePoint.
- Sending alerts when important files are updated.
- Triggering Teams notifications when a task is completed in Planner.

Step 5: SharePoint + Power Apps

Power Apps lets you **build custom forms and apps** that interact directly with SharePoint lists and libraries. This integration allows:

- Easy data entry for non-technical users.
- Custom dashboards and interfaces tailored to your team's needs.
- Mobile access for forms and approvals, making SharePoint more dynamic.

Step 6: SharePoint + Viva Connections

Viva Connections brings your SharePoint content **directly into Microsoft Teams**, giving users a single hub for news, resources, and dashboards. Integration benefits:

- Personalized dashboards for each employee.
- Quick links to SharePoint resources, Planner boards, and team sites.
- Encourages engagement by keeping information accessible where employees spend most of their time—inside Teams.

Step 7: SharePoint + Outlook

SharePoint calendars and tasks can sync with Outlook, allowing users to:

- See project deadlines directly in their calendar.
- Receive notifications and reminders in Outlook when documents are updated.
- Access SharePoint contact lists for efficient communication.

Good to Know: Integration doesn't require advanced IT skills. Most tools offer **built-in connectors**, drag-and-drop web parts, or simple configuration wizards.

Tips for Beginners:

- Start small: Choose one or two integrations (e.g., Teams + SharePoint) and gradually expand.
- Use templates: Microsoft 365 provides prebuilt templates for project management, HR, and department intranets.
- Keep navigation simple: Don't overload your SharePoint site with every app; focus on the tools your team will actually use.
- Educate the team: Offer short guides or training sessions to ensure everyone understands the new workflows.

Watch Out For: Permissions are key. Ensure all users have access to the connected tools; otherwise, integrations can fail or lead to confusion.

Quick Tip: Think of SharePoint as the **control center**, Teams as your **communications hub**, Planner as your **task manager**, OneDrive as your **personal workspace**, and Power Automate/Power Apps as your **workflow and customization tools**. Using them together creates a smooth, efficient, and productive environment.

This integration strategy ensures your team can **collaborate efficiently, stay informed, and make better decisions** using the full power of Microsoft 365.

Chapter 7: Administration and Governance

7.1 SharePoint Admin Center Overview

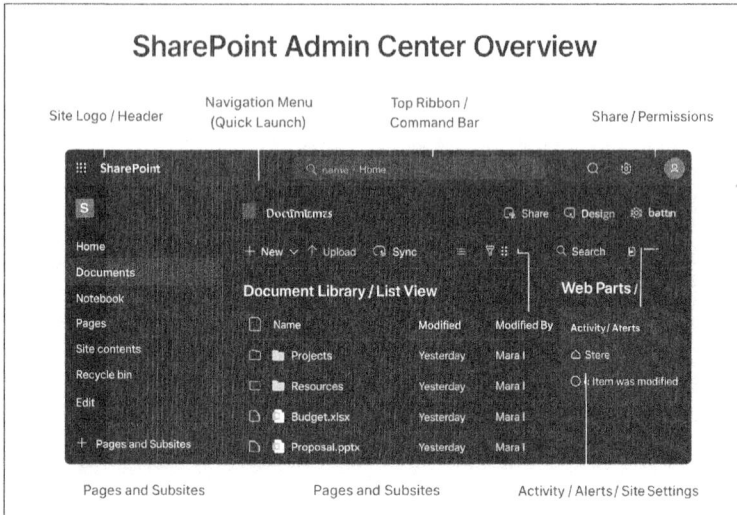

SharePoint Admin Center Overview

The **SharePoint Admin Center** is your command hub for managing and governing SharePoint across your organization. Think of it as the **control room** where administrators can oversee site creation, user permissions, storage, compliance, and overall SharePoint health. Whether you're managing a small team or a large enterprise, understanding the Admin Center is crucial to keeping everything organized, secure, and efficient.

Why the Admin Center Matters

- **Centralized Management:** All sites, libraries, and user settings are in one place, making it easier to monitor activity and enforce policies.
- **Enhanced Security:** Control who has access to what, and set rules to prevent data leaks or unauthorized edits.

- **Performance Oversight:** Track storage usage, site activity, and usage trends to ensure SharePoint runs smoothly.
- **Compliance & Governance:** Ensure your organization adheres to regulatory requirements like GDPR, HIPAA, or internal policies.

Getting Started: Accessing the SharePoint Admin Center

1. Sign in to **Microsoft 365 Admin Center** using your administrator account.
2. Navigate to Admin Centers → SharePoint.
3. You'll see the **SharePoint Admin Center dashboard**, divided into several key sections: Sites, Policies, Sharing, Migration, and Reports.

Main Sections of the Admin Center

1. Active Sites

This is where you can view and manage all SharePoint sites in your organization. Here you can:

- Create new team or communication sites.
- Access site settings, including storage quotas, owners, and permissions.
- Monitor site activity, including the number of active users and last modified files.

Pro Shortcut: Use the search bar to quickly locate a specific site instead of scrolling through the full list.

2. Policies

Policies ensure your organization maintains consistent rules and compliance standards. Within this section, you can:

- Configure sharing settings for internal and external users.
- Set **access control policies**, like limiting external sharing to specific domains.

- Define site classification labels, such as confidential, internal, or public.

Quick Tip: Regularly review your sharing policies to avoid accidental exposure of sensitive data.

3. Sharing

Sharing settings control how users collaborate both inside and outside your organization. Key options include:

- Allowing or blocking external sharing.
- Setting expiration dates for shared links.
- Managing guest user access to specific sites or libraries.

Good to Know: External sharing can be safe if carefully controlled, but always monitor shared links and guest accounts.

4. Migration

The migration section is crucial if you're moving from older SharePoint versions or other platforms. Here, you can:

- Track migration jobs and status.
- Configure migration tools like **SharePoint Migration Tool (SPMT)** or third-party options.
- Ensure metadata, permissions, and file versions are preserved during migration.

5. Reports

Reports give administrators insight into usage patterns, adoption trends, and storage health. For example:

- **Storage Metrics:** See which sites are using the most storage.
- **User Activity:** Identify inactive or highly active users.
- **Sharing Reports:** Monitor external sharing trends and potential risks.

Step-by-Step: Basic Admin Tasks

Creating a New Site

1. Go to **Active Sites** → **Create** → **Team Site or Communication Site**.
2. Enter the **site name, owner, and classification**.
3. Adjust sharing settings as needed.
4. Click **Finish** to create the site.

Managing Permissions

1. Select a site from **Active Sites** → **Permissions**.
2. Add or remove owners, members, and visitors.
3. Use **SharePoint groups** to manage large teams efficiently.

Monitoring Storage

1. Navigate to **Reports** → **Storage Metrics**.
2. Identify sites nearing their storage limits.
3. Archive old files or increase storage quotas if necessary.

Watch Out For: Avoid giving too many users global admin privileges. Only trusted individuals should have full access to prevent accidental changes that could affect the entire organization.

Tips for Beginners:

- Start by exploring one section at a time to avoid feeling overwhelmed.
- Use Microsoft's built-in help links for guided tutorials and explanations.
- Document changes you make in the Admin Center to maintain a record for troubleshooting.
- Encourage your team to follow SharePoint governance guidelines for consistent usage.

Quick Tip: Think of the Admin Center as the **air traffic control for SharePoint**. Just like air traffic controllers ensure planes fly safely and on schedule, administrators use this hub to keep SharePoint sites secure, organized, and running smoothly.

The SharePoint Admin Center is the backbone of your organization's digital workspace. By understanding how to navigate and use it, you can ensure that your team collaborates efficiently, data stays secure, and your SharePoint environment grows in a controlled, structured way.

7.2 Managing Site Collections and Storage

Managing **site collections** and storage in SharePoint is a key responsibility for administrators, as it ensures your organization's data is well-organized, secure, and scalable. Think of site collections as **neighborhoods in a city**, with each site representing a building or office. Proper management ensures everyone can find what they need without overcrowding or running out of space.

What Are Site Collections?

A **site collection** is a group of SharePoint sites that share common settings, permissions, and administration. Each collection has a **top-level site** and can include multiple **subsites**. This structure helps organizations:

- Organize content by department, project, or team.
- Apply consistent policies across related sites.
- Simplify management and reporting.

Why Site Collection Management Matters

- **Efficiency:** Properly structured site collections make it easier for users to navigate and find information.
- **Security:** Centralized permissions reduce the risk of unauthorized access.
- **Storage Control:** Helps avoid exceeding storage quotas and ensures data is not lost or misplaced.
- **Governance:** Ensures compliance with organizational and legal policies.

Step 1: Creating a Site Collection

1. Sign in to the **SharePoint Admin Center**.

2. Click **Active Sites** → **Create** → Team Site or Communication Site.
3. Enter the **site name, description, and owner**.
4. Assign **site classification** (e.g., Internal, Confidential).
5. Review and set **sharing permissions**.
6. Click **Finish**.

Pro Shortcut: Use templates for team sites or communication sites to save time and ensure consistency in layout and features.

Step 2: Managing Existing Site Collections

- **View Site Collections:** In the Admin Center, navigate to **Active Sites** to see all collections.
- **Edit Site Settings:** Select a site collection to update owners, permissions, storage limits, and sharing policies.
- **Monitor Activity:** Track usage and access metrics to identify underused or high-demand sites.

Step 3: Assigning Permissions

- Use **SharePoint groups** like Owners, Members, and Visitors to control access efficiently.
- Avoid assigning permissions directly to individual users for large site collections—it's harder to manage and prone to errors.
- Periodically review permissions to remove inactive users or adjust roles as needed.

Step 4: Managing Storage
Storage management is critical to prevent slow performance or unexpected limits. SharePoint Online allocates storage at the tenant level and distributes it across site collections.

Monitoring Storage:

1. Navigate to **Reports** → **Storage Metrics** in the Admin Center.
2. Check which site collections are consuming the most storage.
3. Identify large files, old versions, or unused content.

Optimizing Storage:

- Enable **versioning** wisely; too many versions of large files can quickly consume storage.
- Encourage users to **archive old documents** in separate storage or download them for long-term storage.
- Use **OneDrive for personal files** and keep SharePoint libraries for shared team documents.

Step 5: Site Collection Lifecycle Management

Managing the lifecycle of site collections ensures your SharePoint environment stays clean and efficient.

Best Practices:

- **Regular Reviews:** Periodically review site collections for activity and relevance.
- **Archiving:** Move inactive or completed project sites to an archive to free up space.
- **Deletion:** Delete unnecessary or redundant site collections following organizational policies.
- **Automation:** Consider using PowerShell scripts or Power Automate to handle repetitive maintenance tasks.

Good to Know: SharePoint Online provides a **Recycle Bin** for deleted sites and content, allowing recovery within a certain retention period. This can prevent accidental loss of important information.

Step 6: Tips for Large Organizations

- **Standardize Naming Conventions:** Helps users identify the purpose of each site collection easily. For example, "HR-Policies" or "Marketing-Campaigns-2025".
- **Plan Hierarchies:** Avoid creating too many subsites; instead, focus on flat site collections for scalability.

- **Delegate Administration:** Assign site collection administrators to manage specific sites while maintaining overall governance at the global admin level.

Quick Tip: Think of storage management like organizing a digital warehouse. If shelves are overfilled, it's hard to find items, and adding new stock becomes difficult. Regularly cleaning and organizing ensures smooth operations.

Watch Out For:

- Assigning too many global admins can lead to unintentional changes across multiple site collections.
- Over-reliance on subsites instead of separate site collections can make permissions and navigation complicated.
- Ignoring storage limits may result in halted uploads or degraded performance.

By effectively managing site collections and storage, you can ensure that your SharePoint environment remains **organized, secure, and efficient**, providing a smooth experience for users and a manageable system for administrators. Proper planning and regular maintenance will prevent issues and support long-term scalability.

7.3 Security and Compliance Essentials

Keeping your SharePoint environment secure while ensuring compliance with organizational policies and legal requirements is a critical responsibility for administrators. Think of it as **locking the doors of a digital office building** while also making sure everyone follows the rules inside. Proper security and compliance measures protect sensitive data, maintain trust, and prevent costly breaches.

Understanding SharePoint Security Layers

SharePoint security is built on multiple layers, each serving a unique purpose:

- **Authentication:** Verifies that a user is who they claim to be. SharePoint Online uses **Microsoft 365 credentials**, supporting Multi-Factor Authentication (MFA) for extra protection.
- **Authorization:** Determines what a verified user can do. Permissions at the site, library, folder, and document levels control actions like view, edit, delete, or share.
- **Data Protection:** Includes encryption at rest and in transit, ensuring that files and communications are secure from unauthorized access.
- **Network Security:** Integration with Microsoft 365's security framework, including firewalls, secure connections (HTTPS), and conditional access policies.

Key Compliance Features in SharePoint

SharePoint provides robust tools to help organizations comply with regulatory and internal policies:

- **Retention Policies:** Automatically retain or delete content based on defined schedules, helping meet **records management requirements**.
- **Data Loss Prevention (DLP):** Prevents sharing of sensitive information like credit card numbers or personal identifiers outside approved users.
- **Audit Logs:** Track who accessed, modified, or deleted content for accountability and reporting.
- **eDiscovery:** Quickly search and export content for legal or regulatory inquiries.

Step 1: Setting Up Permissions Correctly

- Use **SharePoint Groups** like Owners, Members, and Visitors to manage access efficiently.
- Avoid assigning permissions to individual users whenever possible.
- **Quick Tip:** Apply the principle of least privilege—give users only the access they need to perform their tasks.

Step 2: Securing External Sharing

SharePoint allows external users to collaborate, but uncontrolled sharing can create security risks.

- **Restrict access** to specific people or domains.
- Use **expiration dates** for guest access.
- Review external sharing regularly to ensure old links are deactivated.
- **Watch Out For:** Unmonitored sharing links can lead to unintended exposure of confidential data.

Step 3: Enforcing Multi-Factor Authentication (MFA)

MFA adds an extra layer of security by requiring a second verification step, such as a text code or authenticator app.

- Recommended for all users, especially those with admin privileges.
- Helps protect accounts even if passwords are compromised.
- **Good to Know:** MFA can be enforced at the organizational level via Microsoft 365 Security & Compliance settings.

Step 4: Implementing Data Loss Prevention (DLP)

DLP policies scan files for sensitive information and automatically block or warn users before content is shared inappropriately.

- Create policies based on **content type**, such as financial data, personally identifiable information (PII), or health records.
- Educate users on DLP warnings to encourage compliance.
- **Pro Shortcut:** Use templates in Microsoft 365 Compliance Center to quickly set up common DLP policies.

Step 5: Auditing and Monitoring Activity

Regularly monitoring SharePoint usage helps detect unusual behavior and maintain compliance:

- Enable **audit logging** to track activities like file downloads, edits, deletions, and sharing.
- Review logs periodically or use automated alerts for suspicious activity.

- Analyze usage patterns to optimize permissions and site structures.

Step 6: Compliance and Records Management

- Configure **retention labels** to classify documents based on their importance and regulatory requirements.
- Use **information barriers** to restrict communication between certain user groups if required by regulations.
- Apply **legal holds** when content must be preserved for litigation or investigation.

Step 7: Training Users on Security Best Practices

- Conduct regular training sessions for employees about phishing, password hygiene, and secure sharing.
- Encourage users to **report suspicious activity** immediately.
- Provide clear guidance on what types of content can be shared externally and how to use DLP and retention labels.

Quick Tip: Think of SharePoint security like a multi-layered lock system. Even if one layer is bypassed, other layers still protect your content. For example, MFA protects the login, permissions protect access, and DLP ensures sensitive content isn't leaked.

Best Practices for Ongoing Security and Compliance

- **Review permissions regularly:** Remove inactive users and adjust roles as needed.
- **Update policies:** Stay aligned with changing regulations like GDPR, HIPAA, or industry-specific requirements.
- **Test incident response:** Practice what to do if a breach or compliance violation occurs.
- **Automate reporting:** Use SharePoint and Microsoft 365 compliance tools to generate periodic reports for stakeholders.

By following these steps, you ensure your SharePoint environment is **safe, secure, and compliant** while maintaining productivity for your teams.

Proper security and compliance practices protect your organization's data, reduce risk, and foster trust across users, partners, and clients.

7.4 Governance Policies and Naming Standards

Establishing **governance policies** and **naming standards** in SharePoint is like creating a well-organized filing system for a large office building—everything has a place, everyone knows the rules, and nothing gets lost or mismanaged. Without governance, sites, documents, and lists can quickly become chaotic, making collaboration frustrating and increasing the risk of errors or compliance issues.

Why Governance Matters
Governance defines **who can do what, how content is managed, and what rules users should follow**. It ensures:

- Consistency across sites and libraries.
- Security and compliance requirements are met.
- Teams can easily find, share, and manage content.
- Long-term maintainability of your SharePoint environment.

Key Elements of SharePoint Governance

1. **Roles and Responsibilities**

   - Define who can create sites, lists, or document libraries.
   - Assign **Site Owners**, **Site Members**, and **Site Visitors** with clear duties.
   - Determine escalation paths for permissions issues or site management questions.
   - **Quick Tip:** Maintain a central SharePoint admin team to monitor compliance with policies.

2. **Site Lifecycle Management**

   - Define rules for **creating new sites**, including approval workflows.

- ○ Establish **archiving and deletion policies** for old or inactive sites.
- ○ Schedule periodic **site audits** to ensure proper usage.
- ○ **Watch Out For:** Orphaned sites with outdated data that may cause security risks.

3. **Content Management Policies**

- ○ Decide what content types are allowed (documents, spreadsheets, lists, etc.).
- ○ Standardize **metadata** and tagging to improve searchability.
- ○ Implement **retention and disposal policies** to manage document lifecycles.
- ○ **Good to Know:** Metadata-driven content organization improves both usability and compliance.

4. **Security and Permissions Policies**

- ○ Define permission levels for different user roles.
- ○ Establish rules for **external sharing** and guest access.
- ○ Monitor for **broken inheritance** where sub-sites or lists deviate from standard permissions.
- ○ **Pro Shortcut:** Use templates and automated scripts to enforce consistent permissions across new sites.

5. **Naming Conventions**

- ○ Create clear and consistent naming standards for **sites, document libraries, lists, and files**.
- ○ Example: Use prefixes to indicate the department (`HR_`, `FIN_`, `IT_`) and a brief description (`HR_Policies`, `FIN_Reports`).
- ○ Avoid vague or overly long names; clarity makes searching and navigation easier.
- ○ **Quick Tip:** Combine department codes, project names, and dates to standardize files for version tracking (e.g., `IT_ProjectX_2025-10-31_Report.docx`).

6. **Navigation and Hub Site Standards**

   - Define the structure for **hub sites** that connect related team or communication sites.
   - Standardize **navigation menus** for consistency across departments.
   - Implement **homepages and landing pages** with consistent branding and key links.

7. **Training and Communication**

   - Educate users on governance rules, naming conventions, and content standards.
   - Provide **quick reference guides** and **visual examples** for file naming and metadata tagging.
   - Encourage feedback to improve governance processes over time.

Best Practices for Governance and Naming

- Keep rules **simple and clear**—complex policies confuse users.
- Automate enforcement where possible using **Power Automate** or **SharePoint templates**.
- Conduct **regular reviews** to adapt policies as business needs evolve.
- Use **dashboards and reporting** to track adherence to governance standards.
- Promote a **culture of compliance** by recognizing teams that follow standards consistently.

Quick Tip: Think of naming conventions as the labels on a filing cabinet. Even if multiple people are adding documents, a consistent system ensures anyone can find what they need quickly.

Proper governance and naming standards create a SharePoint environment that is **organized, secure, and scalable**. Teams can collaborate efficiently without wasting time searching for files, while administrators can maintain control and ensure compliance.

7.5 Monitoring Site Usage and Analytics

Monitoring site usage and analytics in SharePoint is like keeping an eye on foot traffic in a busy office building—you want to know which areas are most active, where improvements are needed, and how efficiently people are moving through the space. In SharePoint, this "traffic" comes in the form of **site visits, document interactions, user engagement, and workflow activity**. Regular monitoring ensures your SharePoint environment stays efficient, secure, and aligned with business goals.

Why Monitoring Matters
Monitoring site usage and analytics helps you:

- Understand which sites, libraries, and pages are actively used.
- Identify inactive or underutilized resources for archiving or optimization.
- Ensure security and compliance by spotting unusual activity.
- Inform decisions about training, site redesign, or policy updates.
- Measure adoption of SharePoint tools across departments.

Key Metrics to Track

1. **Site Visits and Page Views**

   - Track how many users visit a site and which pages are most popular.
   - Identify trends over time to determine seasonal or project-based usage.
   - **Quick Tip:** Focus on the top pages and libraries to ensure key resources are optimized and easy to access.

2. **Document Interactions**

   - Monitor **uploads, downloads, edits, and shares** for documents.
   - Detect frequently accessed files, which may need more stringent version control or permission checks.

- Watch Out For: Unusual spikes in downloads or shares, which could indicate accidental exposure of sensitive content.

3. **User Activity**

- Identify active users and inactive ones to determine training needs or access adjustments.
- Track **collaboration patterns**, such as frequent co-authoring or commenting.
- **Good to Know:** High collaboration often correlates with better adoption of SharePoint features.

4. **Search Analytics**

- Understand what users are searching for and whether results are relevant.
- Adjust metadata, tagging, and site organization based on search trends.
- **Pro Shortcut:** Use search insights to create shortcuts or highlight content that users frequently seek.

5. **Workflow and Automation Metrics**

- Track completion rates for automated workflows, approvals, or notifications.
- Identify bottlenecks where tasks are delayed or users are not interacting as expected.
- **Quick Tip:** Combine Power Automate analytics with SharePoint site data to get a holistic view of process efficiency.

Tools for Monitoring and Analytics

- **SharePoint Site Usage Reports:** Built-in tools provide insights into site visits, popular content, and user activity.
- **Microsoft 365 Admin Center Reports:** Offers broader analytics across SharePoint, Teams, and OneDrive.
- **Power BI Integration:** Visualize usage patterns, workflow efficiency, and document activity in interactive dashboards.

- **Third-Party Analytics Tools:** Tools like HarePoint or CardioLog Analytics offer advanced monitoring options, including heatmaps, deep user activity logs, and detailed engagement metrics.

Best Practices for Effective Monitoring

1. **Set Clear Objectives**

   - Define what you want to measure—adoption, engagement, compliance, or content relevance.
   - Focus on actionable metrics rather than collecting unnecessary data.

2. **Schedule Regular Reviews**

   - Review analytics weekly or monthly to spot trends early.
   - Combine quantitative data (numbers, metrics) with qualitative feedback from users.

3. **Act on Insights**

   - Use findings to optimize site navigation, reorganize libraries, or archive inactive content.
   - Provide additional training or support where adoption is low.
   - Recognize and reward teams or users with high engagement.

4. **Maintain Privacy and Compliance**

   - Ensure monitoring respects user privacy and complies with organizational policies.
   - Aggregate data where possible to avoid exposing individual user behavior unnecessarily.

5. **Visualize Data for Stakeholders**

   - Present analytics in clear dashboards with charts, graphs, and KPIs.
   - Highlight trends, successes, and areas needing improvement to encourage informed decisions.

Quick Tip: Think of analytics like a fitness tracker for your SharePoint environment. It shows which "muscles" are being used, which areas need more exercise, and how healthy your collaboration ecosystem is overall.

By monitoring site usage and analytics, administrators gain **valuable insights into adoption, performance, and security**, enabling smarter decisions about site management, training, and optimization. A proactive monitoring strategy ensures your SharePoint environment remains **efficient, user-friendly, and aligned with business objectives**.

Chapter 8: Troubleshooting and Optimization

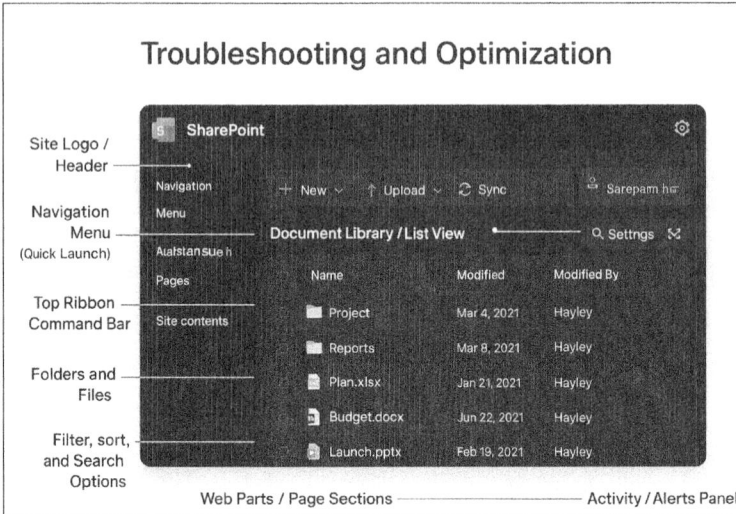

Troubleshooting and Optimization

- Site Logo / Header
- Navigation Menu (Quick Launch)
- Top Ribbon Command Bar
- Folders and Files
- Filter, sort, and Search Options
- Web Parts / Page Sections — Activity / Alerts Panel

8.1 Common SharePoint Errors and Fixes

Navigating SharePoint can sometimes feel like driving through a new city—you might hit a few unexpected bumps along the way. Don't worry! Most errors are common and easy to resolve once you know what to look for. Understanding typical SharePoint issues, their causes, and practical solutions will save time and reduce frustration for both users and administrators.

1. Access Denied Errors

- **What Happens:** Users see a message saying they don't have permission to view a site, document, or library.
- **Common Causes:**
  - ○ Incorrect user permissions.

- ○ Changes in group membership or site inheritance.
- ○ Expired access links.
- **How to Fix:**
  - ○ Check the user's **permissions** in the site settings.
  - ○ Verify that the library or folder is not **breaking permission inheritance** unintentionally.
  - ○ Use **SharePoint Groups** to manage permissions efficiently rather than assigning individually.
- **Quick Tip:** Always explain to users why they might not have access—it avoids confusion and repeated support requests.

2. Page or Web Part Loading Issues

- **What Happens:** Pages fail to load, or web parts display errors.
- **Common Causes:**
  - ○ Browser cache issues.
  - ○ Corrupt web part configurations.
  - ○ Network connectivity problems.
- **How to Fix:**
  - ○ Clear browser cache and refresh the page.
  - ○ Try opening the page in a different browser.
  - ○ Check web part settings in **Edit Mode** and remove or reconfigure faulty web parts.
- **Good to Know:** Modern SharePoint pages are more resilient, but complex scripts or third-party web parts can occasionally cause conflicts.

3. File Upload Failures

- **What Happens:** Users cannot upload files to a library, or uploads stall.
- **Common Causes:**
  - ○ File size exceeds SharePoint limits.
  - ○ Invalid file names (SharePoint has restrictions on certain characters like *, ?, <, >).
  - ○ Browser or network interruptions.

- **How to Fix:**
  - ○ Split large files or use **OneDrive sync** for bulk uploads.
  - ○ Rename files to remove forbidden characters.
  - ○ Confirm network stability and retry.
- **Pro Shortcut:** Use **drag-and-drop** into the library or the **Upload > Folder** option for multiple files.

4. Versioning Conflicts

- **What Happens:** Users see a message about a conflict while saving or editing documents.
- **Common Causes:**
  - ○ Multiple users editing the same document simultaneously.
  - ○ Check-in/check-out requirements not followed.
- **How to Fix:**
  - ○ Enable **co-authoring** features where possible.
  - ○ Encourage users to **refresh the document** before editing.
  - ○ Check the **version history** to resolve conflicts manually.
- **Quick Tip:** For heavily edited files, enable **auto-save and alerts** to keep everyone synchronized.

5. Workflow Failures

- **What Happens:** Automated workflows don't start, stop midway, or produce errors.
- **Common Causes:**
  - ○ Changes in library or list names referenced in the workflow.
  - ○ Permissions issues for workflow initiators or approvers.
  - ○ Power Automate or legacy SharePoint Designer workflows misconfigured.
- **How to Fix:**
  - ○ Verify that the workflow connections are intact.
  - ○ Update actions to reference the correct libraries, lists, or columns.
  - ○ Test the workflow with a small group of users before full deployment.

- **Watch Out For:** Scheduled workflows may fail silently—always review the workflow history for errors.

6. Search Problems

- **What Happens:** Users cannot find documents, lists, or pages.
- **Common Causes:**
  - Content not indexed yet.
  - Permissions restricting visibility.
  - Outdated search schema or crawl errors.
- **How to Fix:**
  - Ensure content is **published** and available to the intended audience.
  - Check search settings in the **SharePoint admin center**.
  - Trigger a manual **reindex** for critical libraries or sites.
- **Good to Know:** SharePoint search indexes content on a schedule, so new files may take time to appear in results.

7. Performance Issues

- **What Happens:** Pages or documents load slowly, or the site feels sluggish.
- **Common Causes:**
  - Large lists or libraries without proper indexing.
  - Excessive custom scripts or complex web parts.
  - Network bandwidth limitations.
- **How to Fix:**
  - Create **indexes** for columns used in filters and views.
  - Optimize web part usage and remove unnecessary custom scripts.
  - Enable **content delivery network (CDN)** features for static assets.
- **Pro Shortcut:** Use **modern pages** wherever possible—they are designed for speed and efficiency.

Tips for Troubleshooting Like a Pro

- **Replicate the Issue:** Try to reproduce the error step-by-step to understand its cause.
- **Use Incognito/Private Mode:** Eliminates browser cache or extension interference.
- **Check Permissions and Inheritance:** Many issues are related to access rights.
- **Leverage SharePoint Health Reports:** Admins can review site health, usage patterns, and errors.
- **Ask for Help Early:** Microsoft 365 Support and community forums are valuable resources.

Quick Tip: Keep a **troubleshooting checklist** for your team. Categorize errors by type, impact, and fix, so issues are resolved faster next time.

By understanding common SharePoint errors and their solutions, you'll be better equipped to **maintain smooth operations, reduce downtime, and improve user satisfaction**. Remember, troubleshooting is part of the learning process, and even seasoned SharePoint administrators encounter hiccups—what matters is knowing where to look and how to act.

8.2 Access and Permission Issues

SharePoint is a powerful collaboration platform, but with great power comes the need for careful access management. Misconfigured permissions are one of the most common challenges users and administrators face. Understanding how access works, common pitfalls, and practical solutions will help you keep your SharePoint environment secure and efficient while ensuring that your team can work smoothly.

Understanding SharePoint Permissions

SharePoint permissions control who can **view, edit, or manage content**. Permissions are applied at different levels:

- **Site Level:** Controls access to the entire site.
- **Library or List Level:** Permissions can be unique or inherited from the site.

- **Folder or Item Level:** Individual files or list items can have specific permissions, though too many exceptions can become confusing.

SharePoint uses **groups and roles** to simplify permissions:

- **Owners:** Full control over the site, including settings and permissions.
- **Members:** Can contribute content (add, edit, delete documents) but cannot change site settings.
- **Visitors:** Read-only access for viewing content.

Common Access Issues and How to Fix Them

1. **Users Cannot Access a Site or Library**

   - **Cause:** The user is not part of the site group or has been removed.
   - **Fix:**
     - Check the **site permissions** via **Settings > Site Permissions**.
     - Add the user to the correct group (Owner, Member, or Visitor).
     - Ensure that the site or library isn't **breaking inheritance** unintentionally.
   - **Quick Tip:** Avoid assigning permissions individually to many users; use groups to simplify management.

2. **"Access Denied" Despite Being a Member**

   - **Cause:** Unique permissions on a subfolder, file, or library override the site permissions.
   - **Fix:**
     - Identify the specific object causing the restriction.
     - Either **re-inherit permissions** from the parent site/library or adjust access explicitly.
   - **Good to Know:** Sometimes SharePoint caches permissions. Have the user **log out and log back in** after adjustments.

3. **External Sharing Issues**

- ○ **Cause:** External users may have received links but lack proper permissions, or external sharing is disabled.
- ○ **Fix:**
  - ▪ Verify **sharing settings** in the SharePoint admin center.
  - ▪ Send **direct invitations** to external users.
  - ▪ Ensure the link type matches the intended access (view-only vs. edit).
- ○ **Watch Out For:** Expired links or links sent to the wrong email address can be a silent source of frustration.

4. **Broken Permission Inheritance**

- ○ **Cause:** When a library, folder, or item has unique permissions, it may not align with site-level expectations.
- ○ **Fix:**
  - ▪ Use **Manage Access** to review where inheritance has been broken.
  - ▪ Decide whether to **keep unique permissions** or **re-inherit** from the parent.
- ○ **Pro Shortcut:** Keep unique permissions to a minimum to simplify troubleshooting.

5. **Issues with Office Integration**

- ○ **Cause:** Users opening files in Word, Excel, or Outlook may encounter errors due to mismatched permissions between SharePoint and Office apps.
- ○ **Fix:**
  - ▪ Ensure the user is **logged into Office with the same Microsoft 365 account**.
  - ▪ Update Office apps to the latest version.
  - ▪ Clear Office credentials and re-authenticate if needed.

Best Practices for Managing Access

- **Use Groups, Not Individuals:** Assign permissions to SharePoint groups instead of individuals to simplify administration.
- **Regularly Review Permissions:** Conduct quarterly audits to remove inactive users and update group memberships.
- **Leverage Microsoft 365 Security & Compliance Center:** Track access and sharing activities to detect unusual behavior.
- **Document Permission Policies:** Keep clear guidelines on who should have access to what to reduce confusion and errors.
- **Educate Users:** Make sure team members understand the difference between view, edit, and owner permissions.

Quick Tip: Use the **"Check Permissions"** feature in SharePoint to see exactly what access a user has. It saves time and prevents guesswork.

Step-by-Step Example: Fixing Access Denied for a Library

1. Navigate to the library where the user cannot access.
2. Click **Settings > Library Settings > Permissions for this document library**.
3. Look for **broken inheritance**. If found, either **re-inherit permissions** or modify the unique permissions.
4. Add the user to the correct SharePoint group or assign permissions directly if necessary.
5. Ask the user to refresh or re-login to confirm access.

Tips for External Users:

- Share links with expiration dates to maintain security.
- Make sure external users have Microsoft accounts to access shared content.
- Use **view-only links** for sensitive documents to reduce risk.

By proactively managing permissions, using groups wisely, and regularly auditing access, SharePoint administrators can ensure both **security and usability**. Remember, most access issues are easy to solve once you understand where the breakdown occurs. Clear communication with users and keeping a **checklist of common fixes** will make your SharePoint environment smooth and frustration-free.

8.3 Performance and Sync Problems

SharePoint is designed to be a robust and scalable platform, but like any complex system, users sometimes experience performance slowdowns or issues with syncing files across devices. Understanding the common causes, practical troubleshooting steps, and preventive measures will help you maintain a smooth experience whether you're accessing SharePoint through the browser, the desktop app, or mobile devices.

Common Performance Issues

Performance problems in SharePoint can show up in several ways:

- Slow page loads or delayed response when navigating sites or libraries.
- Documents taking too long to open, upload, or save.
- Delays in searching or filtering lists and libraries.
- Synchronization lag in OneDrive or SharePoint sync client.

1. Slow Page Loads

- **Causes:**
  - Large lists or libraries with thousands of items.
  - Complex web parts or custom scripts on pages.
  - Network connectivity issues.
- **Solutions:**
  - **Optimize lists and libraries:** Use **folders, metadata, and filtered views** instead of loading thousands of items at once.
  - **Simplify pages:** Remove unused web parts or scripts that add load time.
  - **Check network:** Run a speed test and ensure stable internet. A wired connection often helps.

- **Pro Shortcut:** Use the **"Quick Edit" view sparingly** for very large lists, as it can slow down performance significantly.

2. Document Upload or Download Delays

- **Causes:**
  - Large file sizes or numerous files uploaded at once.
  - Browser caching or outdated versions of Office apps.
  - Antivirus or firewall interference.
- **Solutions:**
  - **Break large uploads into smaller batches.**
  - **Use the OneDrive sync client** to manage files locally and automatically sync changes.
  - Temporarily **disable browser extensions or security software** that may block uploads.
- **Quick Tip:** Ensure files don't exceed SharePoint's file size limit (generally 250GB for modern libraries).

3. Sync Issues with OneDrive or SharePoint Sync Client

- **Causes:**
  - Outdated sync client or Office apps.
  - Conflicts between multiple versions of the same file.
  - Network interruptions during syncing.
- **Solutions:**
  - Keep **OneDrive and Office apps updated**.
  - Check for **sync conflicts** (OneDrive usually flags files with a red icon) and resolve by renaming or merging files.
  - Pause and restart syncing if files appear stuck.
- **Good to Know:** Files with special characters in their names (like \ / : * ? " < > |) may not sync properly. Rename files to remove these characters.

4. Search and Filter Lag

- **Causes:**
  - Very large lists or libraries.

  ○ Non-indexed columns or improperly configured views.
- **Solutions:**
  ○ **Index frequently filtered columns** in large lists.
  ○ Use **filtered views** instead of showing all items at once.
  ○ Consider splitting very large lists into multiple libraries if practical.

5. Browser-Specific Performance Problems

- **Causes:**
  ○ Unsupported browsers or outdated versions.
  ○ Excessive cached data or cookies.
- **Solutions:**
  ○ Use **Microsoft Edge or the latest version of Chrome** for best compatibility.
  ○ Clear cache and cookies if pages are loading incorrectly.
  ○ Disable unnecessary browser extensions that may conflict with SharePoint.

Preventive Measures for Smooth Performance

- **Regularly maintain libraries and lists:** Archive old documents to keep libraries manageable.
- **Monitor site usage:** Identify heavy-traffic pages or libraries and optimize them.
- **Educate users:** Encourage best practices like avoiding extremely large attachments in a single upload and using consistent file naming conventions.
- **Leverage modern SharePoint features:** Modern pages, libraries, and lists are optimized for speed compared to classic pages.

Step-by-Step Example: Resolving a Stuck Sync Issue

1. Open the **OneDrive sync client**.
2. Identify files with a **red x icon** indicating a problem.
3. Right-click the file and select **View online** to see SharePoint's version.

4. Resolve conflicts by renaming files, merging content, or deleting duplicates.
5. Pause syncing for a few minutes, then resume to refresh the process.

Quick Tip: If syncing continues to fail, **unlink and relink your OneDrive account**. This resets the sync connection and often resolves persistent issues.

Pro Shortcut: Use the **"Check Permissions" and "Manage Access" tools** before troubleshooting sync issues. Sometimes delays happen because the user doesn't have the proper access, not because of technical faults.

By understanding the typical causes of performance and sync issues—and applying structured troubleshooting steps—you can prevent frustration, reduce downtime, and keep your SharePoint environment running smoothly. Most problems are fixable with just a few adjustments, so stay proactive and document recurring issues for faster resolution in the future.

8.4 Workflow and Integration Errors

Workflows and integrations are what make SharePoint a truly powerful platform for collaboration and automation. They allow you to automate repetitive tasks, synchronize data between systems, and streamline processes across your organization. However, because these involve multiple systems, apps, and logic steps, errors can occasionally occur. Understanding the common causes, practical solutions, and preventive strategies will help you manage and resolve workflow and integration issues efficiently.

Common Workflow and Integration Issues

Workflow and integration problems in SharePoint often manifest as:

- Workflows failing to start or complete.
- Approval processes getting stuck or not notifying the right users.
- Data inconsistencies between SharePoint and connected apps like Teams, Outlook, or Power Automate.

- Unexpected error messages or failed API calls.
- Delays in task execution or missed triggers.

1. Workflow Failures in Power Automate or SharePoint Designer

- **Causes:**
  - Incorrect configuration of workflow conditions or actions.
  - Missing permissions for users or service accounts.
  - Broken connections to external data sources.
  - Large lists or complex conditions that exceed platform limits.
- **Solutions:**
  - **Check workflow run history:** Power Automate provides detailed logs showing which step failed.
  - **Verify permissions:** Ensure all users involved have the necessary SharePoint access.
  - **Simplify workflows:** Break down very complex workflows into smaller, manageable flows.
  - **Test with sample data:** Before deploying a full workflow, use a small dataset to identify potential errors.
- **Quick Tip:** Use **parallel branches cautiously**—too many simultaneous actions can lead to throttling or timeout errors.

2. Approval and Notification Problems

- **Causes:**
  - Missing or incorrect email addresses in workflow steps.
  - Users not having access to the documents or lists they need to approve.
  - Disabled or misconfigured email settings in Microsoft 365.
- **Solutions:**
  - Double-check the **assigned approvers** in your workflow.
  - Ensure all users have **proper access rights** to the items they need to approve.
  - Test email notifications using a **dummy workflow** to confirm they are sent and received correctly.

- **Good to Know:** Approval emails sometimes land in spam/junk folders, so inform users to check there if expected notifications do not appear.

3. Integration Errors with Other Microsoft 365 Tools

- **Causes:**
  - Outdated connectors or broken API connections between SharePoint, Teams, Planner, or Outlook.
  - Changes in external systems that affect workflow triggers or actions.
  - Rate limits or throttling by Microsoft 365 services.
- **Solutions:**
  - Keep all **connectors up to date**. Microsoft frequently updates connectors to fix bugs.
  - Use **error handling** in your workflows—e.g., "Configure run after" options in Power Automate to handle failures gracefully.
  - Implement **retry policies** for actions that occasionally fail due to temporary system issues.
- **Pro Shortcut:** Use the **Test Flow** feature in Power Automate to simulate workflow execution before deploying to all users.

4. Data Mismatches and Sync Issues

- **Causes:**
  - Differences in data formats or field types between SharePoint and integrated apps.
  - Workflows referencing fields that have been renamed or deleted.
  - Manual edits or external scripts that interfere with workflow logic.
- **Solutions:**
  - Standardize data fields and formats before using them in workflows.
  - Regularly review workflows to ensure all referenced fields and lists exist.

- Implement **data validation rules** in SharePoint lists to prevent incorrect inputs.

5. Common Error Messages and Troubleshooting Steps

- **"Access Denied" Errors:** Check that the workflow account or user has **correct permissions**.
- **"Timeout" or "Action Failed" Errors:** Reduce workflow complexity, split large tasks, or optimize queries.
- **"Connection Not Configured" Errors:** Re-establish broken connectors or update credentials.

Step-by-Step Example: Fixing a Stuck Approval Workflow

1. Open **Power Automate** and locate the workflow in question.
2. Check the **Run History** to identify the step where it failed.
3. Confirm the **approver's email and SharePoint permissions** are correct.
4. If a step involves a large list or library, try **splitting it into smaller batches**.
5. Test the workflow using a **sample item** to ensure it runs smoothly.
6. Republish the workflow once the issue is resolved.

Preventive Measures for Workflow and Integration Success

- **Document workflows:** Keep clear notes on the logic, triggers, and conditions used. This helps when troubleshooting or updating workflows.
- **Regularly review and update:** Microsoft 365 evolves, and so should your workflows. Check them quarterly for broken actions or outdated connectors.
- **User training:** Educate team members on best practices, such as not renaming key columns or moving files mid-process.
- **Error handling:** Implement error handling within workflows to automatically notify admins when failures occur.

Quick Tip: Always **test workflows in a sandbox environment** before rolling them out to the entire organization. This reduces disruption and ensures reliability.

Good to Know: Combining SharePoint workflows with Power Automate provides much greater flexibility than older SharePoint Designer workflows. However, it also introduces new dependencies, so proactive monitoring is key.

By understanding these workflow and integration challenges—and applying structured troubleshooting and preventive strategies—you can ensure SharePoint continues to streamline your organization's processes rather than creating frustration. Remember, most issues are manageable with careful planning, testing, and ongoing monitoring.

8.5 Maintenance and Backup Tips

Maintaining your SharePoint environment and ensuring that your data is safely backed up is essential for smooth operation, preventing data loss, and avoiding disruptions in collaboration. Even if you're a beginner or not very tech-savvy, following simple, structured maintenance and backup routines can save a lot of headaches. Let's dive into practical, detailed guidance on how to keep your SharePoint environment healthy, secure, and efficient.

Why Maintenance Matters

SharePoint is more than just a storage platform—it's a living ecosystem where documents, lists, workflows, and integrations constantly interact. Without regular upkeep, your SharePoint environment can experience:

- Slower performance due to large lists, libraries, or unused items.
- Broken links or workflows caused by moved or deleted files.
- Confusion in site navigation due to outdated pages or cluttered libraries.
- Data loss risks if backups are not maintained or tested.

Daily, Weekly, and Monthly Maintenance Tasks

Daily Checks:

- **Monitor alerts and notifications:** Check any SharePoint alerts for failed workflows or access issues.
- **Review user activity:** Ensure that users are not inadvertently causing conflicts, like multiple versions being edited simultaneously.
- **Quick clean-up:** Remove obvious duplicates or temporary files to keep libraries tidy.

Weekly Tasks:

- **Check storage usage:** Identify sites or libraries nearing quota limits.
- **Review permissions:** Ensure no unintended access changes occurred.
- **Update workflows:** If any automated workflows failed during the week, troubleshoot and fix them promptly.
- **Inspect links and web parts:** Broken links on pages can frustrate users; fix or remove outdated ones.

Monthly Tasks:

- **Audit libraries and lists:** Archive older documents or move them to an archive site to improve performance.
- **Review metadata and tags:** Ensure consistency for better searchability.
- **Test backups:** Periodically restore a small batch of data from your backup to verify that it works correctly.
- **Update SharePoint apps and integrations:** Confirm that connected apps like Teams, Power Automate, and Power Apps are functioning correctly and using updated connectors.

Backup Strategies for SharePoint

Having reliable backups is crucial because even with SharePoint Online's built-in redundancy, mistakes, accidental deletions, or malicious actions can occur. Here's how to approach backups:

1. SharePoint Online Built-in Options:

- **Versioning:** Enable version history for lists and libraries. This allows you to restore previous versions of documents.
- **Recycle Bin:** Deleted items go to the Recycle Bin for 93 days. Administrators can restore items from there if necessary.
- **Retention Policies:** Configure policies to retain content for a specified period even if users delete it.

2. External Backup Tools:

For organizations requiring extra security or regulatory compliance, consider third-party backup solutions. These tools can:

- Backup entire site collections, libraries, or lists.
- Automate scheduled backups.
- Provide point-in-time recovery options.

3. Best Practices for Backups:

- Keep **multiple backup copies** in different locations.
- Test backups periodically to ensure data can be restored.
- Document backup schedules, retention periods, and responsible personnel.
- Use **incremental backups** to save storage space while keeping recent changes.

Maintenance Tips to Keep SharePoint Healthy

- **Optimize Libraries:** Break large libraries into folders or use metadata filters to avoid hitting list view thresholds.
- **Clean Up Sites:** Remove unused pages, apps, and lists that are no longer needed.
- **Update Permissions Regularly:** Remove former employees or redundant groups to maintain security.
- **Document Workflows and Processes:** Clear documentation helps maintain continuity and troubleshoot issues faster.

- **Educate Users:** Encourage users to follow naming conventions, avoid storing unnecessary files, and regularly archive old content.

Pro Shortcut: Use **PowerShell scripts** for bulk maintenance tasks, like checking permissions across multiple sites or cleaning up old versions. This is especially useful for administrators managing large environments.

Good to Know: SharePoint Online is updated automatically by Microsoft, but customizations, integrations, and workflows may need manual maintenance. Keep a list of all custom solutions to ensure they remain compatible after updates.

Quick Tip: Schedule a recurring maintenance day or week in your calendar to ensure that upkeep tasks are consistently performed. Treat it like a health check for your SharePoint environment.

By combining daily vigilance, regular maintenance, and a solid backup strategy, you can keep your SharePoint environment running smoothly, protect valuable organizational data, and provide a seamless experience for your users. A well-maintained SharePoint environment not only improves efficiency but also boosts user confidence and trust in the platform.

Chapter 9: Updates and Best Practices

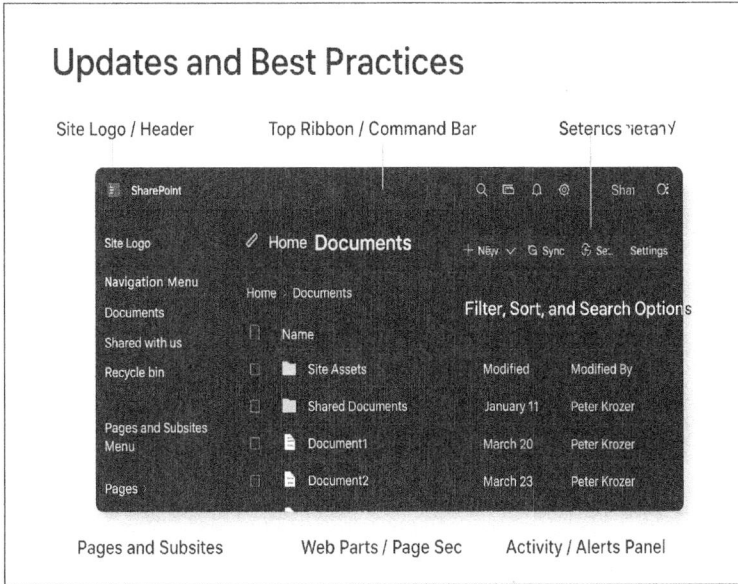

Updates and Best Practices

Site Logo / Header Top Ribbon / Command Bar Seterics ietai̶Y

SharePoint

Site Logo · Home Documents · + New ∨ G Sync G Se Settings

Navigation Menu
Documents
Shared with us
Recycle bin

Home Documents

Name

Filter, Sort, and Search Options

Site Assets

Shared Documents · January 11 · Peter Krozer

Pages and Subsites Menu

Document1 · March 20 · Peter Krozer

Pages

Document2 · March 23 · Peter Krozer

Modified · Modified By

Pages and Subsites · Web Parts / Page Sec · Activity / Alerts Panel

9.1 What's New in SharePoint 2026

SharePoint 2026 introduces an exciting wave of updates designed to make teamwork faster, smarter, and more intuitive than ever before. Whether you're a long-time SharePoint user or just getting started, this release focuses on enhancing user experience, improving collaboration tools, strengthening security, and expanding AI-powered features. The goal is simple: to make managing, sharing, and finding information easier for everyone—no matter your technical skill level.

Let's take a friendly, detailed walk through what's new in SharePoint 2026 and how you can take advantage of its fresh features and improvements.

A More Modern, Intuitive Interface

SharePoint 2026 delivers a cleaner, more user-friendly design that looks and feels like the rest of the Microsoft 365 ecosystem. The navigation has been simplified, with more visual cues, larger icons, and clearer menus to help users find what they need faster.

- **Personalized Dashboards:** Each user now gets a tailored home experience showing recent documents, frequently visited sites, and recommended content—all powered by Microsoft Graph intelligence.
- **Improved Quick Launch Bar:** The left-hand navigation is now customizable, so you can pin your most-used lists, libraries, and pages for quicker access.
- **Responsive Layouts:** Whether you're on a laptop, tablet, or smartphone, the interface adjusts smoothly to fit your screen, improving usability on the go.

Quick Tip: If you're used to the older layouts, don't worry—it may take a few minutes to adjust, but you'll soon find the new design far more intuitive.

AI-Powered Features for Smarter Workflows

Artificial intelligence now plays a bigger role in SharePoint 2026. From intelligent search to automated document summaries, AI helps you spend less time organizing information and more time acting on it.

- **Content Summaries:** AI can now generate short summaries of documents and pages, helping you grasp key points quickly.
- **Intelligent Search:** SharePoint's search engine has been upgraded with semantic understanding—meaning it interprets what you *mean*, not just what you type. For instance, searching for "company guidelines" will also show documents labeled as "policies" or "procedures."
- **Automated Tagging:** Files uploaded to document libraries are automatically tagged using context-aware metadata, making them easier to find later.

- **AI-Powered Insights:** SharePoint surfaces analytics like engagement reports and usage patterns to help you understand which documents or sites are most valuable.

Good to Know: These AI features work behind the scenes. You don't have to turn them on manually—they're built right into your SharePoint environment.

Enhanced Integration with Microsoft 365 Tools

SharePoint 2026 deepens its connection with the rest of Microsoft 365, ensuring seamless transitions between tools like Teams, Outlook, OneDrive, and Viva.

- **Teams + SharePoint Harmony:** Team sites and channels are more tightly linked, allowing files shared in Teams to automatically sync with corresponding SharePoint libraries.
- **Outlook Integration:** You can now save email attachments directly to SharePoint libraries with one click.
- **Viva Connections:** The Viva experience integrates with SharePoint home sites, making internal news and resources accessible directly from Microsoft Teams.
- **Power Platform Expansion:** It's now even easier to build apps (Power Apps) and automate processes (Power Automate) directly within SharePoint, without writing a single line of code.

Pro Shortcut: Try connecting a SharePoint library to Teams using the "Add Cloud Storage" option. It keeps your documents organized and accessible without switching apps.

Stronger Security and Compliance Features

Security remains a top priority in SharePoint 2026. With new compliance options and enhanced data protection tools, organizations can feel confident that their sensitive information is safe.

- **Adaptive Access Policies:** SharePoint now supports conditional access rules based on user behavior, device type, or location. For instance, you can block access to sensitive data from public Wi-Fi networks.

- **Enhanced Data Loss Prevention (DLP):** The new DLP engine can detect more file types and identify potential leaks faster using AI-based pattern recognition.
- **Audit Logs and Compliance Center Integration:** Admins now get detailed activity reports across all connected Microsoft 365 services, simplifying investigations and audits.
- **Granular Sharing Controls:** Admins can restrict sharing by domain or user group, allowing finer control over who can access your content.

Watch Out For: While stronger security is great, some new restrictions might affect how external users interact with shared documents. Always test sharing settings after setup.

Performance and Reliability Upgrades

SharePoint 2026 introduces performance improvements that make loading times snappier and file synchronization more reliable.

- **Faster Page Loads:** Optimized caching and content delivery networks (CDNs) reduce latency, especially for globally distributed teams.
- **Improved File Handling:** Uploads and downloads now support larger file sizes with fewer timeout issues.
- **Offline Sync Improvements:** The OneDrive sync client has been enhanced for smoother offline access to SharePoint content.
- **Background Updates:** SharePoint updates itself quietly in the background, minimizing downtime and user disruption.

Expanded Customization and Design Options

If you love making your sites visually engaging, you'll appreciate the expanded customization capabilities in SharePoint 2026.

- **Modern Themes and Branding:** Choose from a broader palette of color schemes and layout templates to match your organization's brand.
- **Flexible Web Parts:** New web parts include AI summaries, dynamic news feeds, and Power BI integrations for displaying live dashboards.
- **Drag-and-Drop Editing:** Creating or rearranging sections on a page is easier than ever.
- **Template Marketplace:** Microsoft has introduced a library of ready-made templates for intranets, HR portals, and project hubs.

Quick Tip: If you're new to customization, start with Microsoft's prebuilt templates—they're easy to modify and professionally designed.

Improved Collaboration and Co-Authoring

Teamwork is smoother in SharePoint 2026. Multiple users can edit documents simultaneously, comment in real time, and view version histories more clearly.

- **Live Co-Authoring:** Watch others' edits appear instantly on Word, Excel, or PowerPoint documents stored in SharePoint.
- **Comment Threads:** Conversations about specific content stay attached to the document, keeping context intact.
- **Task Integration:** You can now convert comments or discussions into actionable tasks that sync with Microsoft Planner.

User Experience Enhancements for Administrators

Administrators haven't been left out—SharePoint 2026 gives them a more powerful, easier-to-navigate Admin Center.

- **Simplified Controls:** Common settings like permissions, sharing options, and retention policies are now grouped under clearer categories.
- **Centralized Management:** Admins can monitor all site collections, user activities, and storage from one dashboard.

- **Automated Health Reports:** The system automatically identifies potential issues and suggests fixes before users notice them.
- **Role-Based Access:** You can now assign specific management roles (like "Content Manager" or "Workflow Admin") for better control and accountability.

Environmental and Sustainability Updates

Microsoft has committed to sustainability across all its platforms, and SharePoint 2026 plays a role by optimizing server workloads and data efficiency.

- **Greener Data Centers:** SharePoint Online now runs in Microsoft's carbon-negative data centers.
- **Reduced Resource Footprint:** Background processes are more efficient, using less bandwidth and CPU power.
- **User Awareness Tools:** Some dashboards now show the energy impact of file storage and usage patterns—encouraging eco-friendly digital habits.

Good to Know: You don't need to take any action to benefit from these green initiatives—they're automatically included with your Microsoft 365 subscription.

Preparing for the Upgrade

If you're moving from an older version of SharePoint (like 2019 or 2023), transitioning to SharePoint 2026 should be smooth—but a bit of preparation helps.

1. **Back Up Data:** Always back up your current SharePoint content before starting the upgrade process.
2. **Review Custom Solutions:** Ensure that custom workflows or third-party integrations are compatible with SharePoint 2026.
3. **Train Users:** Schedule short workshops or share tutorials to help team members adjust to the new layout and features.

4. **Test Before Rolling Out:** Try the update in a sandbox environment before deploying it organization-wide.

Final Thoughts

SharePoint 2026 represents a thoughtful evolution—making collaboration more intuitive, secure, and intelligent. Whether it's AI-powered assistance, better integration with Microsoft 365, or stronger security, this update is designed to empower users while reducing administrative complexity.

If you've ever found SharePoint overwhelming in the past, this release may be your turning point. It's simpler, smarter, and more human-centered than ever before—truly built for the modern workplace.

Quick Tip: Take time to explore the new features gradually. Start with something simple, like customizing your dashboard or trying out AI search. You'll soon discover that SharePoint 2026 is not just an upgrade—it's a productivity game-changer.

9.2 Transitioning from Older Versions

Moving from an older version of SharePoint—whether it's SharePoint 2013, 2016, 2019, or a legacy on-premises environment—to **SharePoint Online or SharePoint 2026** is a major milestone for any organization. It's not just a technical upgrade; it's a transformation in how teams collaborate, store information, and manage projects in the modern workplace. While the latest SharePoint versions bring enhanced security, automation, and integration with Microsoft 365, the process of transition requires thoughtful planning, careful execution, and strong communication with users. This guide walks you through everything you need to know—from assessing your current environment to ensuring a smooth and confident adoption.

Understanding What's Changing

If you're coming from older SharePoint versions, many aspects will feel different. The biggest shift isn't just in appearance—it's in functionality and design philosophy. Older versions relied heavily on static, hierarchical structures (sites, subsites, and folders). SharePoint Online and SharePoint 2026, on the other hand, embrace **a flat architecture with hub sites**, modern page design, cloud-first storage, and deep integration with Microsoft 365 apps like Teams, Power Automate, and OneDrive.

You'll also notice the move from **classic pages** to **modern pages**, which are faster, responsive, and easier to customize with drag-and-drop web parts. Instead of relying on legacy workflows built with SharePoint Designer or InfoPath, modern SharePoint favors **Power Automate** and **Power Apps** for automation and forms.

Quick Tip: Don't panic if the interface looks unfamiliar—the core concepts (sites, libraries, lists, permissions) are still there, just streamlined and easier to manage.

Step 1: Assess Your Current Environment

Before jumping into migration, take time to understand what you currently have. This assessment phase is crucial for identifying what should be migrated, what can be archived, and what should be rebuilt. Create an inventory of your SharePoint environment, including:

- **Sites and subsites:** Note their purpose, ownership, and last activity date.
- **Document libraries and lists:** Identify critical content and outdated materials.
- **Permissions:** Document who has access to what.
- **Workflows and forms:** List any SharePoint Designer or InfoPath dependencies.
- **Custom code and third-party integrations:** Flag anything that may not be compatible with the new platform.

Good to Know: Microsoft provides tools like the **SharePoint Migration Assessment Tool (SMAT)** to scan your environment and generate detailed reports on potential issues.

Step 2: Choose the Right Migration Path
There's no one-size-fits-all method for upgrading. Your migration path depends on where you're coming from and your organization's needs:

- **Direct migration to SharePoint Online:** Ideal if you're ready to fully embrace the cloud and modernize your workflows.
- **Hybrid migration:** Keeps some content on-premises while moving others online. This is common for organizations with sensitive or regulated data.
- **Manual rebuild:** Sometimes it's best to start fresh. Recreate your critical sites and libraries in SharePoint Online using modern templates instead of migrating legacy clutter.

Watch Out For: Migrating everything "as is" can lead to cluttered, unmanageable environments. Use the transition as an opportunity to **declutter and redesign**.

Step 3: Prepare and Clean Up Content
Before migration, perform a content cleanup. Remove duplicate, outdated, or unused files—often referred to as "ROT" (redundant, obsolete, trivial). Review permissions to ensure only the right users have access. Organize content into logical categories and apply metadata tags for better search and filtering once it's in the new environment.

Pro Shortcut: Use PowerShell scripts or third-party tools like ShareGate or AvePoint to automate bulk cleanups and pre-migration analysis.

Step 4: Map Out Your New Structure
Modern SharePoint encourages a **flat architecture** connected through **hub sites** instead of deep subsite hierarchies. Plan your new structure by grouping sites based on departments, business functions, or projects. For instance:

- Communication sites for company-wide announcements.
- Team sites for collaborative projects.
- Hub sites for linking related areas like HR, Finance, or Marketing.

Quick Tip: Modern navigation is flexible—users can quickly jump between connected sites without getting lost in deep folder trees.

Step 5: Migrate Your Data

Once your structure and cleanup are ready, it's time to move your data. There are several ways to do this:

- **SharePoint Migration Tool (SPMT):** Microsoft's free tool that helps move files, libraries, and lists from on-premises to SharePoint Online.
- **Third-party migration tools:** Platforms like ShareGate, Metalogix, or AvePoint offer more advanced control, reporting, and incremental migration features.
- **Manual upload:** For small teams or minimal content, simply uploading files to the new site might suffice.

Good to Know: Large migrations are often done in **phases** to minimize disruption. You can migrate one department or project site at a time, validating results along the way.

Step 6: Validate and Test Thoroughly

After migration, test everything. Ensure that links, permissions, and workflows work as expected. Check that all content appears correctly and verify metadata consistency. Invite key users (often called "power users") to explore and confirm the setup.

Watch Out For: Broken links and missing documents are common after migration. Tools like ShareGate can automatically report and fix these.

Step 7: Train and Support Your Users

Even the smoothest migration can fail if users aren't properly trained. Introduce your team to the modern SharePoint experience through workshops, videos, or quick-start guides. Focus on showing them the **benefits**—like easier collaboration, better search tools, and integration with Teams and OneDrive.

Quick Tip: Create a "Welcome to the New SharePoint" page with tutorials, FAQs, and support contacts to help users get comfortable.

Step 8: Replace Legacy Workflows and Forms
If you used SharePoint Designer or InfoPath, now's the time to modernize. These tools are deprecated, meaning they won't be supported in future releases. Instead, rebuild workflows using **Power Automate**, and replace InfoPath forms with **Power Apps**. This will not only future-proof your environment but also make automation easier and more powerful.

Pro Shortcut: Microsoft provides templates in Power Automate for common workflows like document approvals, notifications, and data collection.

Step 9: Integrate with Microsoft 365 Apps
SharePoint 2026 thrives within the Microsoft 365 ecosystem. Take advantage of integrations with:

- **Microsoft Teams** for chat-based collaboration.
- **Outlook** for sharing calendar events and announcements.
- **Planner** for task management.
- **Power BI** for data visualization.
  Connecting these tools creates a unified digital workplace that's far more dynamic than traditional file storage.

Good to Know: Teams files are stored in SharePoint libraries by default—so migrating properly ensures seamless future integration.

Step 10: Monitor and Optimize Post-Migration
Once you're up and running, monitor site performance, usage, and adoption rates. Use **SharePoint Admin Center** analytics to see which sites are most active and where users might need more support. Encourage feedback and make small adjustments based on user behavior.

Watch Out For: Don't assume the migration is "done" once files are moved. Continuous optimization keeps the environment healthy and relevant.

Common Challenges and How to Overcome Them

- **Challenge: User resistance to change.**
  Solution: Involve users early, show them time-saving benefits, and provide hands-on training.
- **Challenge: Broken links or missing metadata.**
  Solution: Use pre-migration reports to identify potential issues and correct them before going live.
- **Challenge: Permission confusion.**
  Solution: Simplify permissions by using Microsoft 365 groups instead of nested custom permission sets.
- **Challenge: Workflow compatibility.**
  Solution: Replace legacy workflows with Power Automate and test thoroughly before decommissioning old tools.

Good to Know: Microsoft's cloud-based SharePoint continuously updates, meaning you'll always have access to the latest security, design, and collaboration features—no more manual patching or upgrades.

Encourage Adoption Through Change Management

Migration isn't just technical—it's cultural. People often feel attached to old systems. Communicate early, celebrate small wins, and recognize team members who embrace the new platform. Establish "SharePoint Champions"—enthusiastic users who can help their peers learn and adapt.

Quick Tip: Use SharePoint's built-in analytics to spotlight improvements—for example, how much faster documents are being found or how collaboration has improved.

Long-Term Benefits of Transitioning

Once your migration is complete, you'll enjoy several long-term advantages:

- **Always up to date:** No need for future manual upgrades—SharePoint Online updates automatically.
- **Scalability:** Easily add storage or users as your organization grows.

- **Security:** Enhanced data protection through Microsoft's cloud infrastructure and compliance tools.
- **Integration:** Seamless connection with the rest of Microsoft 365 tools like Teams, Viva, and OneDrive.
- **Accessibility:** Work from anywhere on any device with real-time synchronization.

Final Thoughts

Transitioning from older SharePoint versions to SharePoint 2026 isn't just a system upgrade—it's a business evolution. You're moving from static file management to a living, collaborative ecosystem that connects people, processes, and data seamlessly. With careful planning, clear communication, and ongoing support, your organization can unlock a more productive, flexible, and future-ready workplace.

9.3 Productivity and Collaboration Tips

SharePoint 2026 is more than just a document management system—it's the digital heartbeat of teamwork across Microsoft 365. Whether you're part of a small team or a large enterprise, SharePoint can drastically improve productivity, streamline workflows, and create a more connected organization. However, like any powerful tool, it's not about what it can do—it's about how you use it. This section will walk you through practical, real-world tips to help you and your team get the most out of SharePoint. From collaboration strategies to personalization techniques, you'll discover how to turn your SharePoint environment into a true productivity powerhouse.

Organize Smartly with Clear Site Structures

The way your SharePoint sites are organized directly impacts how efficiently your team can work. Keep your site structure simple and intuitive—avoid creating too many subsites or overly complex navigation paths. Instead, use hub sites to group related sites by department, project, or function. For instance, you might have one hub for "Marketing," another for "Operations," and one for "Projects." Each hub can then host associated team or communication sites. This not only improves discoverability but also ensures consistent branding and permissions.

Quick Tip: Before building new sites, map out your organization's structure. A simple diagram can save you from confusion later.

Use Document Libraries Effectively
Instead of creating endless folders, use **metadata** and **views** to organize files. Metadata—like tags, project names, or document types—lets users filter and find information quickly without clicking through multiple folders. Custom views can display only what's relevant, such as "Documents Modified This Week" or "Pending Approval Files."

Pro Shortcut: Train your team to use "Save As → Sites → [Your SharePoint Site]" directly from Microsoft Word, Excel, or PowerPoint. It saves time and keeps documents centralized.

Enable Real-Time Collaboration
One of SharePoint's biggest strengths is seamless collaboration through Office Online and Microsoft 365 integration. Multiple users can edit the same document at once, see others' changes in real time, and leave comments or suggestions. Encourage team members to use @mentions in comments to notify colleagues directly.

Good to Know: SharePoint automatically saves version histories, so even if multiple people edit a file simultaneously, you can always roll back to an earlier version.

Integrate with Microsoft Teams for Better Communication
SharePoint and Teams work hand in hand—Teams stores its files in SharePoint libraries by default. Encourage users to open documents directly in Teams for quick chats and feedback loops, but switch to SharePoint when they need advanced document management or workflow automation.

Watch Out For: Avoid duplicating content between Teams and SharePoint. Always decide on a single "source of truth" for documents to prevent confusion.

Automate Repetitive Tasks with Power Automate

If you find yourself doing the same steps repeatedly—like sending emails for approvals or moving files between folders—automate them! Power Automate (formerly Microsoft Flow) can handle these processes for you. Create automated workflows such as:

- Send an alert when a file is uploaded to a specific folder.
- Automatically archive documents older than six months.
- Trigger approval requests for new content submissions.

Quick Tip: Start small—automate one or two repetitive tasks first to see immediate time savings.

Encourage Shared Calendars and Task Lists

Keeping everyone aligned is easy when you use SharePoint's built-in calendars and task lists. You can sync them with Outlook or integrate them into Microsoft Planner for visual boards and progress tracking. For large projects, link your SharePoint task list with Planner to ensure accountability and visibility.

Pro Shortcut: Use color-coded categories to mark deadlines, milestones, or team-specific events in shared calendars.

Use News Posts to Keep Everyone Informed

Instead of sending long email chains, use SharePoint's News feature to share updates, project highlights, and announcements. It keeps everyone informed while maintaining a clean record of communications. Pin important news posts to the top of your homepage or create a "What's New" section.

Good to Know: News posts can be rolled up across hub sites, meaning an update published on one site can automatically appear on others within the same department.

Customize Views for Personal Productivity

Encourage team members to personalize their SharePoint experience. For example, a project manager might create a view that shows only "In Progress" tasks, while a designer might view only "Files Awaiting Review." Personalized views prevent information overload and help users focus on what matters most.

Quick Tip: Each user can save their own default view, making their workspace more efficient and tailored to their role.

Use Alerts Wisely

Alerts can keep you informed without needing to constantly check the site. Set alerts for specific lists, libraries, or even individual files so you'll get an email or Teams notification when changes occur.

Watch Out For: Avoid setting too many alerts—you'll end up ignoring them. Instead, choose key areas where you truly need to stay updated.

Encourage Good File Naming Conventions

Simple file names like "Document1" or "New File" create chaos in shared environments. Use descriptive naming conventions that include version numbers or dates (e.g., "Marketing_Plan_Q1_2026_v3.docx"). This helps with searching, sorting, and version tracking.

Good to Know: SharePoint automatically detects duplicate file names and prompts users before overwriting existing documents—another safeguard for version control.

Promote Knowledge Sharing

SharePoint thrives when teams use it as a shared knowledge base. Encourage users to document project learnings, frequently asked questions, or standard procedures in **Wiki Libraries** or **Knowledge Hubs**. This creates a searchable internal knowledge base that new employees can benefit from immediately.

Pro Shortcut: Use page templates for recurring documentation types like "How-To Guides" or "Project Reports" to save time.

Leverage Search and Filters

SharePoint's search capabilities are incredibly powerful—especially when content is well-tagged. Teach users to use filters, refiners, and keyword queries. You can even enable "People Search" to find colleagues by expertise, department, or location.

Quick Tip: Use the "Pin to Top" feature in search results to highlight frequently used resources or official templates.

Collaborate Across Departments with Hub Sites

Hub sites bring together multiple related sites under a unified structure. For example, a "Product Development Hub" can connect R&D, Marketing, and QA sites, enabling cross-team visibility. Each site can share navigation, branding, and search—making interdepartmental collaboration seamless.

Watch Out For: Don't create too many hubs. Each should serve a clear, strategic purpose—otherwise, navigation becomes fragmented.

Train and Support Users Continuously

Even with an intuitive platform, users need guidance. Offer short training sessions or internal webinars on SharePoint best practices. Create a "Help & Support" page with quick-start guides, FAQs, and short explainer videos.

Good to Know: Microsoft frequently updates SharePoint features. Keeping your team informed about new tools helps maintain enthusiasm and efficiency.

Embrace Mobile Access

SharePoint's mobile app ensures your team stays connected on the go. You can view documents, read announcements, and collaborate without needing your laptop. This is especially useful for remote teams or field workers.

Quick Tip: Pin your most-used sites to your mobile app's homepage for one-tap access.

Encourage Feedback and Continuous Improvement

No system is perfect from day one. Encourage team members to share suggestions for improving site layouts, navigation, or workflows. You can even create a feedback form within SharePoint using Microsoft Forms or Lists.

Pro Shortcut: Automate feedback collection—set a workflow that notifies the site owner whenever new feedback is submitted.

Maintain a Balance Between Structure and Flexibility
While governance and policies are important, don't over-restrict users. Give teams enough flexibility to create pages, lists, and workflows that meet their daily needs while ensuring consistency and compliance through well-defined templates and permissions.

Good to Know: Empowered users are engaged users—when people feel trusted to shape their digital workspace, adoption and productivity soar.

In Summary
Boosting productivity in SharePoint isn't about learning every feature—it's about using the right ones the right way. Keep your site structure clear, promote collaboration through shared tools, automate repetitive tasks, and always keep communication transparent. With a few smart habits and a culture of sharing, your organization can transform SharePoint from a simple document repository into a dynamic hub of creativity, coordination, and connection.

9.4 Future Microsoft 365 Integrations

As Microsoft continues to evolve its ecosystem, SharePoint remains at the center of collaboration, document management, and workflow automation. Looking ahead, the future of SharePoint within Microsoft 365 is all about **deep integration**, **intelligent automation**, and **seamless user experience**. Understanding where these innovations are heading will help you stay one step ahead and make the most of your SharePoint investment.

Tighter Integration with Microsoft Copilot
One of the biggest trends shaping SharePoint's future is the integration of **Microsoft Copilot**, the AI-powered assistant across Microsoft 365 apps.

Copilot is being built directly into SharePoint to help users summarize long documents, draft pages automatically, and even suggest layouts or metadata tags for uploaded files. Imagine asking Copilot, "Summarize all Q3 project updates in this document library," and getting a clean summary instantly. This level of automation will transform how teams interact with information—making SharePoint not just a storage hub but a smart workspace that works *with* you.

Unified Search and Data Experience

Microsoft's **Graph-powered search** is expected to become more intelligent and personalized. Future updates will make it possible to search across Teams chats, Outlook emails, SharePoint libraries, and even OneDrive files in a single, unified experience. For example, you could type "budget proposal" into SharePoint's search bar and get results from related Teams threads, Planner tasks, and Excel sheets—all neatly organized by relevance.

Deeper Teams and Viva Integration

SharePoint and Teams already work hand-in-hand, but Microsoft is taking that relationship further. In upcoming versions, **Teams channels will have richer, SharePoint-powered experiences**—like dynamic dashboards, embedded workflows, and more flexible document libraries directly inside Teams. Similarly, **Microsoft Viva** (the employee experience platform) will continue to rely heavily on SharePoint for delivering knowledge, learning materials, and internal communications. Viva Topics, for instance, will use SharePoint's AI-driven knowledge graphs to surface expertise and insights across your organization.

Low-Code and No-Code Expansion

Microsoft's Power Platform (Power Apps, Power Automate, and Power BI) will continue to integrate more closely with SharePoint. The goal is to make **automation and app-building accessible to everyone**, not just developers. Soon, you'll be able to launch automated workflows or design data-driven dashboards right from your document library without switching tools. Expect **more templates, pre-built connectors**, and

AI-assisted app creation that tie SharePoint data directly into business solutions.

Enhanced Security and Compliance Tools

With data privacy laws evolving globally, Microsoft is focusing on **proactive compliance** and **data lifecycle management**. Future SharePoint updates will likely include smarter data classification systems, automatic sensitivity labeling, and improved threat protection for files shared internally and externally. These features will help organizations manage risk while maintaining productivity—a key concern for IT administrators and compliance officers alike.

Extended API and Integration Ecosystem

For developers and IT professionals, Microsoft is expanding SharePoint's **API surface** and enhancing compatibility with **Graph API** and **PowerShell**. This means more flexibility for integrating SharePoint with external systems like CRMs, HR platforms, or third-party analytics tools. Expect simplified authentication models and greater automation potential for cross-platform operations.

Hybrid and Edge Enhancements

While SharePoint Online continues to dominate, Microsoft isn't leaving hybrid users behind. Improved **hybrid search**, **content synchronization**, and **edge caching** options will allow on-premises systems to integrate more naturally with the cloud. This ensures businesses with regulatory or infrastructure constraints can still benefit from cloud innovation without compromising control.

AI-Powered Content Lifecycle Management

Artificial intelligence is becoming the backbone of SharePoint's content strategy. In the near future, SharePoint will use AI not only to tag and organize files but to predict their usefulness and suggest archiving or deletion when content becomes outdated. This reduces clutter and helps teams maintain a clean, efficient digital workspace.

Good to Know: Microsoft has announced that future iterations of SharePoint will focus on **adaptive design**—meaning your sites will automatically adjust layouts, colors, and accessibility features based on user preferences and device type. This is great news for organizations with diverse workforces and varying technical abilities.

Quick Tip: Stay updated with Microsoft's **SharePoint Roadmap** and **Microsoft 365 Message Center**. These tools show upcoming changes, rollout timelines, and previews of new features—so your team can prepare and train users in advance.

Pro Shortcut: Join Microsoft's **SharePoint Community Hub** or **Tech Community forums**. These spaces are perfect for discovering early previews, asking questions, and learning from real-world implementations of future integrations.

Final Thoughts
The future of SharePoint within Microsoft 365 is bright and evolving rapidly. As AI becomes more integrated, users can expect a smarter, more connected, and more personalized experience. The key to success will be embracing these updates gradually—experimenting with features like Copilot, Viva, and Power Automate to see how they fit your team's workflow. Don't feel pressured to adopt everything at once; instead, take it one step at a time. The beauty of SharePoint is that it grows with you—adapting to your organization's needs while empowering you to collaborate, innovate, and stay ahead in the digital workspace of tomorrow.

9.5 Recommended Resources and Learning Paths

Staying up to date with SharePoint, especially as Microsoft rolls out new features and integrations in 2026, can feel overwhelming. Don't worry—there's a wealth of resources and learning paths designed to help beginners, non-technical users, and seasoned professionals alike. With the right guidance, you can confidently navigate SharePoint's updates, improve collaboration, and become a power user in your organization.

Official Microsoft Learning Platforms
Microsoft offers a comprehensive set of learning resources specifically for SharePoint and Microsoft 365. The **Microsoft Learn** platform is an

excellent starting point. It provides step-by-step tutorials, interactive exercises, and guided learning paths for topics such as document management, site creation, security, and automation. For example, the learning path *"SharePoint Online for Beginners"* walks users through building team sites, managing libraries, and customizing pages in a structured, easy-to-follow format.

Microsoft Docs and Tech Community

For more detailed, technical guidance, **Microsoft Docs** is the official documentation repository. It includes articles, best practices, API references, and troubleshooting tips. If you prefer a community-driven approach, the **Microsoft Tech Community** is a vibrant hub where users share tips, ask questions, and provide real-world solutions. Engaging in forums can also expose you to use cases you might not have considered, such as integrating SharePoint with Power Automate workflows or using AI-powered search features.

Instructor-Led Training and Certifications

For learners who benefit from structured, guided instruction, Microsoft offers instructor-led training courses. These are ideal for organizations training multiple team members simultaneously. Additionally, pursuing certifications like **Microsoft 365 Certified: Teamwork Administrator Associate** can validate your skills and give you confidence when managing SharePoint sites and permissions. These certifications also help IT teams standardize practices and ensure security and compliance.

YouTube Tutorials and Video Courses

Many professionals find video tutorials helpful for visual learning. Channels such as **Microsoft Mechanics**, **Collab365**, and independent SharePoint educators provide video demonstrations on creating pages, automating workflows, and leveraging new features. Video tutorials are especially useful for seeing features in action, such as drag-and-drop web parts, custom lists, and live co-authoring.

Books and eBooks

Books remain a reliable resource for in-depth learning. Titles like *"SharePoint 2026 For Dummies"*, *"Mastering SharePoint Online"*, and *"Practical SharePoint: Collaboration, Automation, and Governance"* provide structured learning that's easy to digest. These books often include real-world examples, screenshots, and step-by-step exercises that reinforce hands-on practice.

Podcasts and Webinars

For learners who prefer audio or live sessions, podcasts and webinars are valuable. Programs like **SharePoint Shepherds**, **CollabTalk Podcast**, and webinars hosted by Microsoft or MVPs (Most Valuable Professionals) cover updates, trends, and best practices. Listening while commuting or during breaks can help reinforce knowledge and inspire new ways to use SharePoint effectively.

Learning Path Recommendations

To build a comprehensive understanding of SharePoint, consider following a structured learning path:

- **Beginner Level:** Focus on site navigation, creating pages, document libraries, and basic permissions. Use Microsoft Learn modules and beginner-friendly YouTube tutorials.
- **Intermediate Level:** Dive into lists, metadata, workflows with Power Automate, and integration with Teams and Outlook. Explore hands-on labs and community forums.
- **Advanced Level:** Explore governance, security, compliance, custom development, and multi-site management. Consider certifications, advanced courses, and community events.

Quick Tip: Keep a **learning journal** to track features you've mastered and areas you want to explore. This practice helps reinforce knowledge and allows you to reference tips quickly when working on your SharePoint sites.

Pro Shortcut: Join local or virtual **SharePoint user groups**. Networking with peers often accelerates learning and provides insights into how organizations of similar size and industry use SharePoint to solve real problems.

Good to Know: Microsoft periodically updates its learning paths and resources to reflect new features. Regularly checking **Microsoft Learn** ensures your knowledge remains current and aligned with SharePoint 2026 capabilities.

Final Thoughts

Investing time in the right resources and following a structured learning path will make SharePoint approachable and even enjoyable. Start with foundational skills, gradually explore integrations, and embrace community support. With consistent practice and engagement, you'll not only stay up to date with Microsoft 365 but also gain confidence in leveraging SharePoint to enhance collaboration, productivity, and organizational efficiency. Remember, learning SharePoint is a journey—you don't have to know everything at once. Take it step by step, celebrate small wins, and you'll become a SharePoint pro in no time.

Printed in Dunstable, United Kingdom

75486571R00100